Mastering phpMyAdmin for Effective MySQL Management

Marc Delisle

Mastering phpMyAdmin for Effective MySQL Management

Copyright © 2004 Packt Publishing

First Updated: October 2004

Published by Packt Publishing Ltd.
32 Lincoln Road
Olton
Birmingham, B27 6PA, UK.

ISBN 1-904811-03-5

www.packtpub.com

Cover Design by www.visionwt.com

Credits

Author
Marc Delisle

Technical Reviewer
Garvin Hicking
Alexander Turek

Commissioning Editor
Louay Fatoohi

Technical Editor
Niranjan Jahagirdar

Layout
Niranjan Jahagirdar

Indexers
Vijay Tase
Ashutosh Pande

Proofreader
Chris Smith

Cover Designer
Helen Wood

About the Author

Marc Delisle started to contribute to phpMyAdmin in December 1998, when he made the first multi-language version. He has been actively involved since May 2001 as a developer and project administrator. phpMyAdmin is now a part of his life.

He has worked since 1980 at Collège de Sherbrooke, Québec, Canada, as an application programmer and network manager. He has also been teaching networking, security, Linux servers, and PHP/MySQL application development. In one of his classes, he was pleased to meet a phpMyAdmin user from Argentina.

I am truly grateful to Louay Fatoohi, my editor, who approached me for this book project, and accompanied me during the production; his sound comments were greatly appreciated. My thanks also go to Garvin Hicking, a member of the phpMyAdmin's development team and the reviewer for this book. Garvin's sharp eye helped in making this book clearer and more complete.

Finally, there would be no book about phpMyAdmin without phpMyAdmin (the software). I wish to thank all contributors to the source code and documentation; the time they gave to the software project still inspires me and continues to push me forward.

To Carole, André, Corinne, Annie, and Guillaume, with all my love.

About the Reviewers

Garvin Hicking is a German webdeveloper working for Faktor E GmbH. He creates web applications using PHP and MySQL, and in his free time enjoys working on open source projects like phpMyAdmin or Serendipity. When he's away from the computer, he likes going to the movies with his girlfriend and friends, blogging, and taking pictures. What he enjoys most about his work in Open Source is to make people's everyday life easier, by giving them free, but powerful, tools to play with. Receiving feedback of satisfied users is one of the fundamental *give and get* principles he likes to live by.

Alexander Marcus Turek was born on June 2nd, 1984 in Düsseldorf, the capital of the German province Northrhine-Westphalia. Currently, he's studying *Information Engineering and Management* at the University of Karlsruhe, but his origin is Mülheim an der Ruhr, the home of his family. He first got in touch with the Web in 1998, when he won a 28.8k modem at the *CeBit Home* in Hannover, Germany. A few months later, he learned HTML and started his first Web project, a German game patch archive called *Rabus' Update Site*, which he renamed to `bugfixes.info`, when the `.info` domains became available. In the meantime, he switched from static HTML to PHP in order to be able to manage the growing archive more efficiently. He kept on learning PHP when trying to extend the portal.

Because the flatfile-based database system became too slow when searching the still growing archive, he also switched to MySQL in 2001. This is when he got in touch with phpMyAdmin and the project. He started with revising their language files because they were a bit outdated and inconsistent. He had fun doing so, and continued with grabbing some bug reports and submitting patches for them. Loïc Chapeaux, one of the two co-maintainers at that time, added him to the developers list and gave him a CVS account in March 2002, in March 2002, so he could merge his patches by himself. Since then, he mainly worked on the compatibility with MySQL 4.0, reworked the server administration area, developed a simple abstraction layer in order to support MySQLi, and continued with compatibility fixing—this time for MySQL 4.1 and 5.0.

Unfortunately, phpMyAdmin and his studies became too time consuming, and so he had to stop working on `bugfixes.info` in 2003.

Table of Contents

Introduction

Used by millions of developers, MySQL is the most popular Open Source database, supporting numerous large dynamic web sites and applications. MySQL has acquired this wide popularity by virtue of its open source nature, reliability, robustness, and support for various platforms.

This popularity has also been aided by the existence of **phpMyAdmin**, the industry-standard administration tool that makes database management easy for both the experienced developer and novice. The powerful graphical interface that it provides to MySQL has made phpMyAdmin an indispensable tool for MySQL and Web developers.

This book is a comprehensive tutorial to phpMyAdmin, demonstrating the full potential of this tool. It shows how to configure, activate, and use phpMyAdmin's myriad features, both basic and advanced.

What This Book Covers

This is a quick review of the eighteen chapters of the book.

Chapter 1 is an introduction to phpMyAdmin, its history, and main features. *Chapter 2* provides detailed coverage of the different installation and configuration options, including installing one copy of phpMyAdmin for multiple users, and configuring it to manage up to three different servers. Security issues are also discussed in this chapter.

Chapter 3 is an overview of the graphical interface of phpMyAdmin. A more detailed examination of the various panels and windows is provided in the following chapters. In *Chapter 4* we see how to create our first database and table and its various fields. Deleting single and multiple rows, tables, and databases is covered in *Chapter 5*. This chapter also covers data-editing operations, such as handling Null values and applying MySQL functions to data.

Chapter 6 focuses on the various options of phpMyAdmin for changing table structure. These include adding field types such as TEXT, BLOB, ENUM, and SET, uploading binary data into BLOB fields, and managing indexes. phpMyAdmin can be used to backup data and take intermediary snapshots during development and production phases. *Chapter 7* shows how to perform these tasks using the export feature of phpMyAdmin. The various data formats that can be exported are also explained.

phpMyAdmin can also import data, which is the focus of *Chapter 8*. Importing SQL and CVS files, and phpMyAdmin's handing of compressed files are covered here. In addition to its user friendly browsing features, phpMyAdmin allows us to easily search through our data. *Chapter 9* covers searching databases and single tables.

The previous chapters dealt mostly with table fields. *Chapter 10* focuses on operations that affect tables as a whole. Repairing and optimizing tables, changing the various table attributes, and copying and moving tables to another database are all explained.

In *Chapter 11*, we start reading about phpMyAdmin's more advanced features. We see how to install the linked-tables infrastructure, which is required for using various advanced features. Both single- and multi-user installations are covered. Defining inter-table relations is also explained.

In addition to letting us perform various database operations through its graphical interface, phpMyAdmin also allows us to run complex SQL commands for tasks that cannot be performed through the graphical interface. This feature is covered in *Chapter 12*. *Chapter 13*, which covers multi-table search, complements *Chapter 9* and shows how to search single tables and a whole database.

Chapter 14 covers phpMyAdmin's powerful feature of query bookmarks, which is one of the linked-tables features that were covered in Chapter 11. The chapter shows how to record, manipulate, and pass parameters to bookmarks.

Creating and maintaining good documentation about data structure is crucial, particularly for team projects. phpMyAdmin allows us to do this, and this feature is covered in *Chapter 15*. The chapter shows how to generate simple table and column lists, use data dictionaries for complete column lists, and generate custom-made relational schema for tables in the PDF format.

phpMyAdmin can perform MIME-based transformation on column contents. Transformation of both text and images is covered in *Chapter 16*. *Chapter 17* covers character sets and collations in detail.

Chapter 18 shows how system administrators can use phpMyAdmin for user account and privileges management and server status verification.

Chapter 19, the last chapter of the book, covers various troubleshooting and support issues. It covers the most common error messages and configuration problems. The chapter also includes information on how and where you can get technical support.

What You Need to Use This Book

You need to have access to a server or workstation that has the following installed:

- MySQL
- PHP
- Apache or IIS Web server

2

Conventions

In this book you will find a number of styles of text that distinguish between different kinds of information. Here are some examples of these styles, and an explanation of their meaning.

There are three styles for code. Code appearing within text is shown as follows: "The $cfg['PropertiesIconic']$ parameter can have the values TRUE, FALSE, or 'both'".

Blocks of code are set like this:

```
$cfg['PropertiesIconic']    = TRUE;
$cfg['ModifyDeleteAtLeft']  = TRUE;
$cfg['ModifyDeleteAtRight'] = FALSE;
```

When we wish to draw your attention to a particular part of a code block, the relevant lines will be set in bold type:

```
CREATE TABLE `books` (
  `isbn` varchar(25) NOT NULL default '',
  `author_id` int(11) NOT NULL default '0',
  PRIMARY KEY   (`isbn`),
  KEY `author_id` (`author_id`)
) TYPE=MyISAM COMMENT='Contains book description';
```

New terms and **important words** are introduced in a bold-type font. Words that you see on the screen, in menus or dialog boxes for example, appear in our text like this: "clicking the Next button moves you onto the next screen".

> Tips, suggestions, and important notes appear in a box like this.

Any command-line input and output is written as below:

```
c:\packt>mysqladmin ping
mysqld is alive
```

Reader Feedback

Feedback from our readers is always warmly welcomed. Let us know what you think about this book, what you liked or may have disliked. Reader feedback is important for us to develop titles that you really get the most out from.

To send us general feedback, simply drop us an e-mail to feedback@packtpub.com, making sure to mention the book title in the subject of your message.

If there is a book that you need and would like to see us publish, then please send us a note in the Suggest a title form on www.packtpub.com or e-mail suggest@packtpub.com.

If there is a topic that you have expertise in, and you are interested in either writing or contributing to a book, then see our author guide on www.packtpub.com/authors.

Customer Support

Now that you are the proud owner of a Packt book, we have a number of things for you to get the most from your purchase.

Downloading the Example Code for the Book

Visit http://www.packtpub.com/support, and select this book from the title list to download any example code or extra resources for this book. The files available for download will then be displayed.

> The downloadable files contain instructions on how to use them.

Errata

Although we have taken every care to ensure the accuracy of our contents, mistakes do happen. If you find a mistake in one of our books—maybe a mistake in text or a code error, we would be grateful if you could report this to us. By doing this you can save other readers from frustration, and also help to improve subsequent versions of this book.

If you find any errata, you can report them by visiting http://www.packtpub.com/support, selecting your book, clicking on the Add Errata link, and entering the details of your errata. Once your errata have been verified, your submission will be accepted and the errata added to the list of existing errata. The existing errata can also be viewed from the same page by clicking on the View Errata.

Questions

You can contact us at questions@packtpub.com if you are having a problem with some aspect of the book and we will do our best to address it.

Introducing phpMyAdmin

Welcome to the evolved Web! In the last few years, the Web has changed dramatically. In its infancy, the Web was a medium used mainly to convey **static** information ("Look, my home page is on the Web!"). Now, large parts of the Web carry information that is **dynamically generated** by application programs, on which enterprises and even individuals rely for their intranets and public websites.

Because of the clear benefits of databases (better accessibility and structuring of information), web applications are mostly database driven. The front end used is the well known (and quickly deployed) web browser, and there is a database system at the backend. Application programs provide the interface between the browser and the database.

Those who are not operating a database-driven website today are not using the medium to its fullest capability. Also, they could be lagging behind competitors who have made the switch. So it is not a question of whether we *should* implement a database-driven site, but it is more about *when* and mostly *how* to implement it.

Why web applications? They improve user experience and involve them in the process by opening up possibilities such as:

- Gathering feedback about the site
- Letting users communicate with us and with each other through forums
- Ordering goods from our e-commerce site
- Enabling easily editable web-based information (content management)
- Designing and maintaining databases from the Web

Nowadays, WWW might stand for **World-Wide Wave**, a big wave that profoundly modifies the way developers think about user interface, data presentation, and, most of all, the way data reaches users and comes back to the data center.

PHP and MySQL: The Leading Open-Source Duo

This chapter describes the place of phpMyAdmin in the context of PHP/MySQL, explains phpMyAdmin's history, and summarizes its features. Let us look at the solutions currently offered by host providers. The most prevalent is the PHP/MySQL combination.

Well supported by their respective home sites, `http://www.php.net` and `http://www.mysql.com`, this duo has enabled developers to offer a lot of readymade open-source web applications, and most importantly, enabled in-house developers to quickly put in place solid web solutions.

MySQL, which is mostly compliant with the ANSI-92 SQL standard, is a database system well known for its speed, robustness, and small connection overhead, which is important in a web context where pages must be served as quickly as possible.

PHP, installed as a module inside the web server, is a popular scripting language in which applications are written to communicate with MySQL on the backend, and browsers on the front. Ironically, the acronym's signification has evolved itself along with the Web evolution, from **Personal Home Page** to **Professional Home Page**, to its current recursive definition: **PHP: Hypertext Processor**. Available on millions of Web domains, it drives its own wave of quickly developed applications.

What Is phpMyAdmin?

phpMyAdmin is a web application written in PHP and contains XHTML, CSS, and JavaScript client code. It provides a complete web interface to administering MySQL databases and is widely recognized as the leading application in this domain.

Being open source since the start of its existence, it has enjoyed support from numerous developers and translators world wide (being translated into 47 languages at the time of going to press). The project is currently hosted on SourceForge.

Host providers everywhere have shown their trust in phpMyAdmin (official home page at `http://www.phpmyadmin.net`) by installing it on their servers. In addition, we can install our own copy of phpMyAdmin inside our web space, as long as our provider has installed the minimum PHP version required by phpMyAdmin, which is currently PHP 4.1.0. Moreover, the web server must have access to a MySQL server (version 3.23.32 or later)—either locally or on a remote machine. The popular CPanel (a website control application) interfaces with phpMyAdmin.

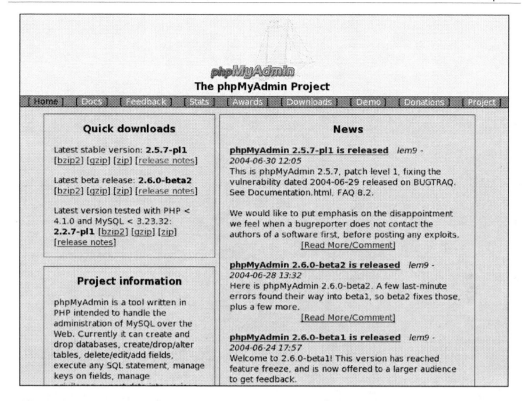

History

The first internal version (0.9.0) was coded by Tobias Ratschiller and bears the date 09-09-1998. He then released version 1.0.1 on 10-26-1998. The early versions were offered on Tobias's site: http://www.phpwizard.net (this site is no longer associated with him). As Tobias wrote in the accompanying notes:

> "This work is based on Peter Kuppelwieser's MySQL-Webadmin. It was his idea to create a web-based interface to MySQL using PHP3. Although I have not used any of his source-code, there are some concepts I've borrowed from him. phpMyAdmin was created because Peter told me he wasn't going to further develop his (great) tool."

Compared to today's version (six years after the original), the first version was somewhat limited in features, but could nonetheless be used to create databases and tables, edit their structure, and enter and retrieve data. Notice in the figure that follows that the left frame was already there to list database names (not table names yet), and the right frame was the workspace to manage a database or table.

This is what the interface for databases looked like in version 1.3.0:

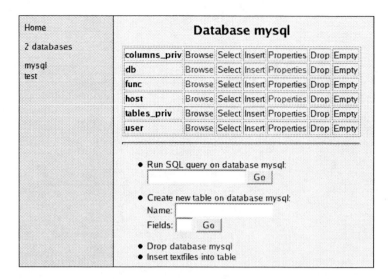

To work on a table, you had the following screen:

I started using phpMyAdmin at version 1.2.0 (released 11-29-1998) and was immediately hooked on to the idea of being able to use a web application to maintain a remote database. However, students at Collège de Sherbrooke, where I work in Québec, Canada, are French-speaking folks, so I contacted Tobias and offered to transform his source code by outsourcing all messages in a message file. He accepted the offer and I created the English and the French message files. Then, on 12-27-1998, Tobias released version 1.3.1, the first multi-language version (meanwhile, he had managed to create the German message file).

In 1999 and the first half of 2000, Tobias improved the navigation system, added features, and merged more language files. His project site maintained a discussion forum, so new ideas came along and patches were discussed. Version 2.1.0 was released on 08-06-2000, which was the last version released by Tobias, who had no more time to devote to this project.

However, users were already numerous, and asked more of the product. Patches were floating on the Internet, with no way of coordinating them. A security alert (and fix) had been published, but no new version was being released. On 03-31-2001, Olivier Müller registered the phpMyAdmin project on SourceForge.net, and released a 2.2.0pre1 version. At this time, this was called the *unofficial* version. This restart of the project attracted some developers, who now had the SourceForge infrastructure (CVS server, forums, bug trackers, mailing lists) to help speed up the development. I personally 're-joined' the project in May 2001 and started fixing and improving the code, as my co-developers were doing.

We became 'official' on 05-28-2001, as Tobias accepted our new version as the new official one. I remember those months of a very intense development effort, with daily improvements and bug fixes, along with new documentation sections. This effort culminated on 08-31-2001 with the release of version 2.2.0.

Here's an excerpt from the announcement file for 2.2.0:

"After 5 months, 5 beta releases, and 4 release candidate versions, the phpMyAdmin developers are pleased to announce the availability of phpMyAdmin 2.2.0. [...] on 31st March 2001, Olivier Müller (Switzerland), supported by Marc Delisle (Québec), Loïc Chapeaux (France) and a team of 8 other developers re-started the phpmyadmin project on SourceForge.net, with the authorization of the original package maintainer. And now, after 5 months of patches, bugfixes, new features and testing, the version 2.2.0 is finally ready."

This version had security fixes, seven new languages (with dynamic language-detection), and the code had been reworked to be CSS2 and XHTML 1.0 compliant, and follow the PEAR coding guidelines. The bookmarks feature appeared in this version.

During the following year the development continued with the release of seven minor versions. The last version of the 2.2.x series is 2.2.7-pl1, which is also the last to have been fully tested under PHP 3. A date to note: 04-03-2002; we registered phpmyadmin.net as the official domain for the project.

On 08-11-2002, version 2.3.0 was released. There had been so many new features that the pages were getting vertically too big, so this version was the 'great split version', displaying sub-pages for each table and database group of features.

The team started a new schedule of releasing a new minor version (2.3.1, 2.3.2 ...) every two months. On 02-23-2003, version 2.4.0 included a new server/user management facility. Then on 05-11-2003, version number jumped to 2.5.0 to celebrate the new MIME-type cell transformation system.

The current version, 2.6.0, supports the new `mysqli` extension available in PHP 5, for better performance and improved security. The interface for this version has been redesigned, including new icons and a theme manager. All these features are explained in this book.

phpMyAdmin has also won some awards, as can be seen in the Awards section on the project's home page. First, it was awarded 'Project Of The Month' for December 2002 by the administrators of SourceForge. In the interview-style document we prepared to put on the SourceForge POTM page, I wrote that I was impressed by the download rate of our product, which was three per minute at that time (since then we have reached ten per minute on peak days).

phpMyAdmin received 75% of the votes from the readers of both the German *PHP Magazin* and its international version, in the category 'Best PHP Application/Tool' for 2003. This award was officially presented at the 2003 International PHP Conference in November 2003.

phpMyAdmin Features Summary

The goal of phpMyAdmin is to offer complete web-based management of MySQL servers and data, and to keep up with MySQL and web standards evolution. While the product is not perfect, it currently includes the most commonly requested features and lots of extras.

The development team constantly develops the product based on the reported bugs and requested features, regularly releasing new versions at intervals of about two months.

phpMyAdmin offers features that cover basic MySQL database and table operations. It also has an internal relational system that maintains metadata to support advanced features. Finally, system administrators can manage users and privileges from phpMyAdmin. It is important to note that phpMyAdmin's choice of available operations depends on the rights the user has on a specific MySQL server.

The basic features consist of

- Database creation and deletion
- Table creation, renaming, copying, and deletion
- Table structure maintenance, including indexes
- Special table operations (repair, optimization, changing type)
- Data insertion, modification, deletion
- Data display in horizontal/vertical mode, and Print view
- Data navigation and sorting
- Binary data uploading

- Data search (table or database)
- Querying by example (multi-table)
- Batch-loading of data
- Exporting structure and data in various formats, with compression
- Multi-user and multi-server installation

The advanced features include:

- Field-level comments
- Foreign keys (with or without InnoDB)
- Browse foreign table
- Bookmarks of queries
- Data dictionary
- PDF relational schema and dictionary
- SQL queries history
- Connection to MySQL using either the traditional `mysql` extension or the new `mysqli` extension (in PHP 5)
- Character set support for databases, tables, and fields (with MySQL 4.1)
- Column contents transformation based on MIME type
- Theme management to customize the interface's look

The server administration features consist of:

- User and privileges management
- Database privileges check
- Server status
- Full server export

Summary

This chapter talked about:

- How the Web has evolved as a means to easily deliver applications
- Why we should use PHP/MySQL to develop these applications
- How phpMyAdmin is recognized as a leading application to interface MySQL from the Web
- The history of phpMyAdmin
- A brief list of its features

Installing phpMyAdmin

It's time to install the product (there are various ways to do so) and to configure it minimally for first-time use.

We may install phpMyAdmin for the following reasons:

- Our host provider did not install a central copy
- Our provider installed it, but the version installed is not current
- We are working directly on our enterprise's web server

Some host providers offer an integrated web panel where we can manage accounts, including MySQL accounts, and also a file manager that can be used to upload web content. Depending on this, the mechanism we use to transfer phpMyAdmin to our web space will vary. We will need some specific information before starting the installation:

- The web server's name or address. Here, we will assume it is www.mydomain.com.
- Our web server's account information (username, password), which will be used either for FTP or SFTP transfer, SSH login, or web control panel login.
- The MySQL server's name or address. Often this is localhost, which means it is located on the same machine as the web server. We will assume this to be mysql.mydomain.com.
- Our MySQL server's account information (username, password).

Download Phase

There are various files available in the Downloads section of http://www.phpmyadmin.net. There might be more that one version offered here; always download the latest stable version. We only need to download one file, which includes all the language files and works regardless of the platform (browser, web server, MySQL, or PHP version).

However, for PHP, if we are using a server supporting only PHP3, we will have to download a file with .php3 in its name. In this case, while following the present instructions, we will have to transpose to .php3 each time we talk about .php files.

The files offered have various extensions: .zip, .bz2, .gz. Download a file having an extension for which you have the corresponding extractor. .zip is the most universal file format in the Windows world, although it is bigger than .gz or .bz2 (common in the Linux/Unix world).

After clicking on the appropriate file, we will have to choose the nearest mirror. The file will start to download, and we can save it on our computer.

The next step depends on the platform you are using; the coming sections detail the procedure for some common platforms. You may proceed directly to the relevant section.

Installation on Remote Linux Servers Using a Windows Client

Using the File explorer, we double-click the phpMyAdmin-xxx file (where xxx represents the version) downloaded on the Windows machine; a file extractor should start, showing us all the scripts and directories inside a main phpMyAdmin-xxx directory, as shown here using **PowerArchiver**:

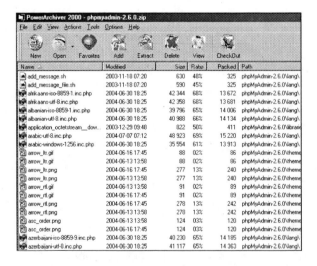

Use whatever mechanism your file extractor offers to save all the files, including subdirectories, to some location on your workstation. Here, we have chosen c:\, so a c:\phpMyAdmin-xxx directory has been created for extraction.

Now, we have to open the config.inc.php file located in the newly created directory.

This file contains special characters (Unix-style end of lines), so we must open it with a text editor that understands this format. If we use the wrong text editor, this file will be displayed with very long lines.

The best choice is a standard PHP editor. Another choice would be **WordPad** or **UltraEdit**, but we should be careful not to add any characters (even blank lines) at the beginning or end of the file. This would disturb the execution of phpMyAdmin and generate the Cannot send header output... error message. If this happens, refer to Chapter 19 for *Troubleshooting and Support*.

Now that the file is open, we go to the *Basic Configuration* section and follow the instructions there. We save our file (in text format), and then come back here.

Now it's time to transfer the whole directory structure c:\phpMyAdmin-xxx to the web server, into our web space. We use our favorite FTP software or the web control panel for the transfer.

The exact directory under which we transfer phpMyAdmin may vary: it could be our public_html directory or another directory where we usually transfer web documents.

Each time the config.inc.php modified, it will have to be transferred again to our web space. This transfer might have to be done explicitly with a specific transfer program, or might be a feature of an editor like HomeSite, Komodo, or PHPEdit, which can save directly via the FTP protocol.

Installation on Local Linux Servers

Let's say we chose phpMyAdmin-xxx in .gz format and downloaded it directly to some directory on the Linux server. We move it to our web server's document root directory (for example, /var/www/html) or to one of its subdirectories (for example, /var/www/html/utilities). Then we extract it with the following shell command or any graphical file extractor our window manager offers:

```
tar -xzvf phpMyAdmin-x.x.x-php.tar.gz
```

We ensure that the permissions and ownership of the directory and files are appropriate for our web server; the web server user or group must be able to read them.

Then we use a text editor to open the config.inc.php file located in the newly created directory.

> Be careful not to add any blank line at the beginning or end of the file; this would hamper the execution of phpMyAdmin.

Now that the file is open, move on to the *Basic Configuration* section in this chapter.

Installation on Local Windows Servers (Apache, IIS)

The procedure here is similar to that described in the *Installation on Remote Linux Servers Using a Windows Client* section, except that the target directory will be under our DocumentRoot (for Apache) or our wwwroot (for IIS). Of course, we do not need to transfer anything after the modifications of config.inc.php, as the directory is already on the web space.

Apache is usually run as a service, so we have to ensure that the user under which the service is running has normal read privileges to access our newly created directory. The same principle applies to IIS, which uses the IUSR_machinename user. This user *must* have read access to the directory. You can adjust permissions in the Security/permissions tab in the directory's properties.

Basic Configuration

> Before configuring, we can rename the directory phpMyAdmin-x.x.x to something easier to remember, like phpMyAdmin, phpmyadmin, admin, or whatever. This way, we or our users will be able to visit an easily remembered URL to start phpMyAdmin.

The config.inc.php File

Let's now have a look at the config.inc.php file. This file contains valid PHP code, defining the majority of the parameters (expressed by PHP variables) that we can change to tune phpMyAdmin to our own needs. There are also normal PHP comments in it, and we can comment our changes.

Starting with phpMyAdmin 2.6.0, there is another configuration file: layout.inc.php. As this version offers theme management, this file contains the theme-specific colors and settings. There is one layout.inc.php per theme, located in themes/themename, for example, themes/original. We will cover the modification of some of those parameters in Chapter 4 on *First Steps*).

In this section, we explain only the parameters we need to change in order to get phpMyAdmin working. Other parameters will be discussed in the chapters where the corresponding features are explained.

The original config.inc.php contains parameter values that enable a login to a MySQL server running on the localhost server with a username of root and no password. This is the default setup produced by most MySQL installation procedures, even if this is not really secure. But if our freshly installed MySQL server still has the default root account, we will be able to login easily and see a warning given by phpMyAdmin about such lack of security.

PmaAbsoluteUri

The first parameter to have a look at is $cfg['PmaAbsoluteUri'] = '';

In most cases we can leave this one empty, as phpMyAdmin tries to auto-detect the correct value. If later we browse a table and then edit a row and click Save, we will receive an error message indicating that we must put the correct value in this parameter.

For example, we would change it to:

```
$cfg['PmaAbsoluteUri'] = 'http://www.mydomain.com/phpMyAdmin_2.5.4/';
```

Then, we would change this other parameter, replacing FALSE with TRUE:

```
$cfg['PmaAbsoluteUri_DisableWarning'] = TRUE;
```

This will remove a warning message that we would have seen when starting phpMyAdmin, and prove that we took care of the absolute URI parameter.

Server-Specific Sections

The next section of the file contains server-specific configurations, each starting with:

```
$i++;
$cfg['Servers'][$i]['host']             = '';
```

If we examine only the normal server parameters (other parameters will be covered starting with Chapter 11), we see for each server a section like the following:

```
$i++;
$cfg['Servers'][$i]['host']          = '';
$cfg['Servers'][$i]['port']          = '';
$cfg['Servers'][$i]['socket']        = '';
$cfg['Servers'][$i]['connect_type']  = 'tcp';
$cfg['Servers'][$i]['extension']     = 'mysql';
$cfg['Servers'][$i]['compress']      = FALSE;
$cfg['Servers'][$i]['controluser']   = '';
$cfg['Servers'][$i]['controlpass']   = '';
$cfg['Servers'][$i]['auth_type']     = 'config';
$cfg['Servers'][$i]['user']          = 'root';
$cfg['Servers'][$i]['password']      = '';
$cfg['Servers'][$i]['only_db']       = '';
$cfg['Servers'][$i]['verbose']       = '';
```

In this section, we have to enter in $cfg['Servers'][$i]['host'] the hostname or IP address of the MySQL server; for example, mysql.mydomain.com or localhost. If this server is running on a non-standard port or socket, we fill in the correct values in $cfg['Servers'][$i]['port'] or $cfg['Servers'][$i]['socket']. See the section on connect_type for more details about socket.

The displayed server name inside phpMyAdmin's interface will be the one entered in 'host' (unless we enter a non-blank value in the following parameter). For example:

```
$cfg['Servers'][$i]['verbose'] = 'Test server';
```

This feature can thus be used to hide the real server hostname as seen by the users.

extension

The traditional mechanism by which PHP can communicate with a MySQL server, as available in PHP before version 5, is the mysql extension. This extension is still available in PHP 5, but a new one called mysqli has been developed and should be preferred for PHP 5, because of its improved performance and its support of the full functionality of MySQL family 4.1.x. This extension is designed to work with MySQL version 4.1.3 and higher.

In phpMyAdmin version 2.6.0, a new library has been implemented, making possible the use of both extensions—choosing either for a particular server. We indicate in $cfg['Servers'][$i]['extension'] the extension we want to use.

Another important parameter (which is not server specific but applies to all server definitions) is $cfg['PersistentConnections']. For all servers to which we connect using the mysql extension, this parameter, when set to TRUE, instructs PHP to keep the connection to the MySQL server open. This speeds up the interaction between PHP and MySQL. However, it is set to FALSE by default in config.inc.php, because persistent connections are often a cause of resource depletion on servers—MySQL refusing new connections. For this reason, the option is not even available for the mysqli extension.

connect_type

Both the mysql and mysqli extensions automatically use a socket to connect to MySQL if the server is on localhost. Consider this configuration:

```
$cfg['Servers'][$i]['host']          = 'localhost';
$cfg['Servers'][$i]['port']          = '';
$cfg['Servers'][$i]['socket']        = '';
$cfg['Servers'][$i]['connect_type']  = 'tcp';
$cfg['Servers'][$i]['extension']     = 'mysql';
```

The default value for connect_type is 'tcp'. However, the extension will use a socket because it concludes that this is more efficient as the host is localhost, so in this case, we can use tcp or socket as the connect_type. To force a real tcp connection, we can specify 127.0.0.1 instead of localhost in the host parameter. Because the socket parameter is empty, the extension will try the default socket. If this default socket, as defined in php.ini, does not correspond to the real socket assigned to the MySQL server, we have to put the socket name (for example, /tmp/mysql.sock) in $cfg['Servers'][$i]['socket'].

If the hostname is not localhost, a tcp connection will occur—here, on the special port 3307. However, leaving the port value empty would use the default 3306 port:

```
$cfg['Servers'][$i]['host']    = 'mysql.domain.com';
$cfg['Servers'][$i]['port']    = '3307';
$cfg['Servers'][$i]['socket']  = '';
```

```
$cfg['Servers'][$i]['connect_type']    = 'tcp';
$cfg['Servers'][$i]['extension']       = 'mysql';
```

compress Configuration

Starting with PHP 4.3.0 and MySQL 3.23.49, the protocol used to communicate between PHP and MySQL allows a compressed mode. Using this mode provides better efficiency. To take advantage of this mode, simply specify:

```
$cfg['Servers'][$i]['compress']        = TRUE;
```

Authentication Type: config

For our first test, we will use the config authentication type, which is easy to understand. However, in the *Multi-User Installation* section, we will see more powerful and versatile ways of authenticating.

Although it seems that we are logging in to phpMyAdmin, we are not! The authentication system is a function of the MySQL server. We are merely using phpMyAdmin (which is running on the web server) as an interface that sends our user and password information to the MySQL server. Strictly speaking, we do not log in *to* phpMyAdmin but *through* phpMyAdmin.

> Using the config authentication type leaves our phpMyAdmin open to intrusion, unless we protect it as explained in the *Security* section of this chapter.

We enter here our username and password for this MySQL server:

```
$cfg['Servers'][$i]['user']            = 'marc';
$cfg['Servers'][$i]['password']        = 'bingo';
```

We can then save the changes we made in config.inc.php.

Testing Basic Configuration

Now it's time to start phpMyAdmin for the first time. This will test the following:

- The values we entered in the config file
- The setup of the PHP component inside the web server
- Communication between web and MySQL servers

We start our browser and point it to the directory where we installed phpMyAdmin, as in http://www.mydomain.com/phpMyAdmin. If this does not work, we try http://www.mydomain.com/phpMyAdmin/index.php (this would mean that our Web server is not configured to interpret index.php as the default starting document).

If you still get an error, refer to Chapter 19, *Troubleshooting and Support*.

We should now see phpMyAdmin's home page. Chapter 3 gives an overview of the panels seen now.

Multi-Server Configuration

The original config.inc.php file has three server-specific sections, enabling a single copy of phpMyAdmin to manage three different servers, but we can add sections to manage more. Let us see how to configure more servers.

Servers Defined in the Configuration File

In the server-specific sections of the config.inc.php file, we see lines referring to $cfg['Servers'][$i] for each server. Here, the variable $i is used so that one can easily cut and paste whole sections of the configuration file, to configure more servers.

Then, at the end of the sections, the following line controls what happens at startup:

```
$cfg['ServerDefault'] = 1;
```

The default value, 1, means that phpMyAdmin will connect by itself to the first server defined. We can specify any number, for the corresponding server-specific section. We can also enter the value 0, signifying no default server, in which case phpMyAdmin will present a server choice:

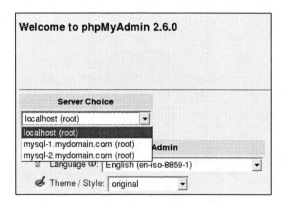

Arbitrary Server

Another mechanism can be used if we want to be able to connect to an undefined MySQL server. First we have to set the following parameter:

```
$cfg['AllowArbitraryServer']    = TRUE;
```

Then, we need to use the cookie authentication type, explained in the next section. We will be able to choose the server and enter a username and a password.

> This mechanism should probably be used in conjunction with a reinforced
> security mechanism (see the *Security* section), because any MySQL server
> accessible from our web server could be connected to.

As seen here, we still can choose one of the defined servers in Server Choice, but we can
enter an arbitrary server name, a username, and a password:

Multi-User Installation

We might want to allow a single copy of phpMyAdmin to be used by a group of persons,
each having their own MySQL username and password, seeing only the databases they
have rights to. Or we might prefer to avoid having our username and password in clear
text in config.inc.php.

Authentication Types Offered

Instead of relying on a username/password pair stored in config.inc.php, phpMyAdmin
will communicate with the browser and get authentication data from it. This enables **true
login** for all users defined in a specific MySQL server, without having to define them in
the configuration file. There are two modes offered that allow a controlled login to
MySQL via phpMyAdmin: http and cookie. We will have to choose the one that suits
our specific situation and environment (more on this in a moment). Both modes require
that we first define a control user.

The Control User

To be able to use authentication types for every kind of MySQL user (in MySQL, user privileges may be expressed in various ways), we should define a control user and password in the server-specific section of a server. If we do not define one, users who have been defined in MySQL with a syntax of 'user'@'hostname' or 'user'@'%' will be able to login, and others won't.

The control user is a special user (the usual name we choose for it is pma, a familiar abbreviation for phpMyAdmin) who has the rights to read some fields in the special mysql database (which contains all the user definitions). phpMyAdmin sends queries with this special control user only for the specific needs of authentication, and not for normal operation. The commands to create the control user are available in phpMyAdmin's Documentation.html, and may vary from version to version. This documentation contains the most current commands.

There is another reason to define a control user: to be able to use the advanced relational features of phpMyAdmin.

When our control user is defined, we fill in the parameters as in the following example:

```
$cfg['Servers'][$i]['controluser']    = 'pma';
$cfg['Servers'][$i]['controlpass']    = 'bingo';
```

I use the bingo password when I teach phpMyAdmin; it is recommended to avoid using the same password for your own installation.

HTTP Authentication

This mode, http, is the traditional mode offered in HTTP, in which the browser asks for the username and password, sends them to phpMyAdmin, and keeps sending them until all the browser's windows are closed.

To enable this mode, we simply use the following line:

```
$cfg['Servers'][$i]['auth_type']      = 'http';
```

This mode has some limitations:

- PHP, depending on the version, might not support HTTP authentication. It works when PHP is running as a module under Apache; for other cases, we should consult the PHP documentation for our version.
- If we want to protect phpMyAdmin's directory with a .htaccess file (see the *Security* section in this chapter), this will interfere with HTTP authentication type; we cannot use both.

There is not a true logout; we will have to close all browser windows to be able to log in again with the same username. Even considering those limitations, this mode may be a valuable choice for the following reasons:

- It does not require the browser to accept cookies.
- Some browsers (like Mozilla) can store the authentication information in an encrypted form.
- It is a bit faster than cookie processing.

Cookie Authentication

The other mode, cookie, presents a login panel (see the following figure) from within phpMyAdmin. This can be customized since we have the application source code. However, as you may have guessed, for cookie authentication, the browser must accept cookies coming from the web server:

This mode stores the username typed in the login screen into a permanent cookie in our browser. The password is stored as a temporary cookie. In a multi-server configuration, the username/password pair corresponding to each server is stored separately. To protect the username/password secrecy against some attack methods that target cookie content, they are encrypted using the Blowfish mechanism. So, to use this mode, we have to define (once) in config.inc.php a secret password that will be used to securely encrypt all passwords stored as cookies from this phpMyAdmin installation.

This is done by putting a secret password here:

```
$cfg['blowfish_secret'] = 'SantaLivesInCanada';
```

Then, for each server-specific section, use the following:

```
$cfg['Servers'][$i]['auth_type']       = 'cookie';
```

23

The next time we start phpMyAdmin, we will see the login panel.

By default, phpMyAdmin displays (in the login panel) the last username for which a successful login was achieved for this particular server, as retrieved from the permanent cookie. If this behavior is not acceptable (we would prefer that someone else who logs in from the same workstation should not see the previous username), we can set the following parameter to FALSE:

```
$cfg['LoginCookieRecall']        = FALSE;
```

A security feature was added in phpMyAdmin 2.6.0: a time limit for the validity of the entered password. This feature helps to protect the working session. After a successful login, our password is stored in a cookie, along with a timer. Every action in phpMyAdmin resets the timer. If we stay *inactive* a certain number of seconds, as defined in $cfg['LoginCookieValidity'], we are disconnected and have to log in again. The default is 1800 seconds. The cookie authentication mode is superior to http in terms of the functionalities offered. It offers true login and logout, and can be used with PHP running on any kind of web server.

Security

Security can be examined at various levels:

- Directory-level protection for phpMyAdmin
- IP-based access control
- The databases that a legitimate user can see
- In-transit data protection

Directory-Level Protection

Suppose an unauthorized person is trying to execute our copy of phpMyAdmin. If we used the simple config authentication type, anyone knowing the URL of our phpMyAdmin will have the same effective rights on our data as us. In this case, we should use the directory-protection mechanism offered by our web server (for example, htaccess) to add a level of protection.

If we chose to use http or cookie authentication types, our data would be safe enough, but we should take the normal precautions with our password (including its periodic change).

The directory where phpMyAdmin is installed contains sensitive data. Not only the configuration file, but ultimately all scripts stored there must be protected from alteration. We should ensure that apart from us, only the web server effective user has read access to the files contained in this directory, and only we can *write* to them.

phpMyAdmin's scripts never have to modify anything inside this directory, except when we use the Save export file to server feature, explained in Chapter 7.

Another possible attack is from other developers having an account on the same web server as us. In this kind of attack, someone can try to open our config.inc.php file. Since this file is readable by the web server, someone could try to include our file from their PHP scripts. To guard against this, we should ensure with our provider that the PHP safe mode is active.

IP-Based Access Control

An additional level of protection can be added, this time verifying the **Internet Protocol (IP)** address of the machine from which the request to use phpMyAdmin is received.

To achieve this level of protection, we construct rules allowing or denying access, and specify the order in which these rules will be applied.

Rules

The format of a rule is:

```
<'allow' | 'deny'> <username> [from] <source>
```

from being optional. Here are some examples:

```
allow Bob from 1.2.3.4
```

User Bob is allowed access from IP address 1.2.3.4.

```
allow Bob from 1.2.3/24
```

User Bob is allowed from any address matching the network 1.2.3 (this is CIDR IP matching).

```
deny Alice from 4.5/16
```

User Alice cannot access when located on network 4.5.

```
allow Melanie from all
```

User Melanie can login from anywhere.

```
allow Julie from localhost
```

Equivalent to 127.0.0.1

```
deny % from all
```

all can be used as an equivalent to 0.0.0.0/0, meaning any host.

Usually we will have several rules. Let's say we wish to have the two rules that follow:

```
allow Marc from 45.34.23.12
allow Melanie from all
```

We have to put them in `config.inc.php` (in the related server-specific section) as follows:

```
$cfg['Servers'][$i]['AllowDeny']['rules'] =
   array('allow Marc from 45.34.23.12',
      'allow Melanie from all');
```

When defining a single rule or multiple rules, a PHP `array()` is used, and we must follow its syntax, enclosing each complete rule within single quotes, and separating each rule from the next with a comma.

The next parameter explains the order in which rules are interpreted.

Order of Interpretation for Rules

Be default, this parameter is empty:

```
$cfg['Servers'][$i]['AllowDeny']['order'] = '';
```

This means that *no* IP-based verification is made.

Suppose we want to allow access by default, but deny access only to some username/IP pairs. We should use:

```
$cfg['Servers'][$i]['AllowDeny']['order'] = 'deny,allow';
```

In this case, all deny rules will be applied first, followed by `allow` rules. If a case is not mentioned in the rules, access is granted. Being more restrictive, we'd want to deny by default. We can use:

```
$cfg['Servers'][$i]['AllowDeny']['order'] = 'allow,deny';
```

This time, all `allow` rules are applied first, followed by deny rules. If a case is not mentioned in the rules, access is denied.

The third (and most restrictive) way of specifying rules order is:

```
$cfg['Servers'][$i]['AllowDeny']['order'] = 'explicit';
```

deny rules are applied before `allow` rules, but to be accepted, a username/IP address *must be listed* in the allow rules and not in the deny rules.

Restricting the List of Databases

Sometimes it is useful to avoid showing in the left panel all the databases to which a user has access. In this case, the `only_db` parameter can be used. It may contain a database name or a list of database names. Only these databases will be seen in the left panel:

```
$cfg['Servers'][$i]['only_db']          = 'payroll';
$cfg['Servers'][$i]['only_db']          = array('payroll', 'hr');
```

The database names can contain MySQL wildcard characters like _ and %.

This parameter applies to all users for this server-specific configuration.

> This mechanism does not replace the MySQL privilege system. Users' rights on
> other databases still apply, but they cannot use phpMyAdmin's left panel to
> navigate to their other databases or tables.

Protecting In-Transit Data

The HTTP protocol is not inherently immune to network sniffing (grabbing sensitive data
off the wire), so if we want to protect not only our username and password but all the
data that travels between our web server and browser, we have to use HTTPS.

To do so, assuming that our web server supports HTTPS, we just have to start
phpMyAdmin by putting https instead of http in the URL, as follows:

```
https://www.mydomain.com/phpMyAdmin
```

If we are using PmaAbsoluteUri auto-detection:

```
$cfg['PmaAbsoluteUri'] = '';
```

phpMyAdmin will see that we are using HTTPS in the URL and react accordingly. If not,
we must put the https part in this parameter, as follows:

```
$cfg['PmaAbsoluteUri'] = 'https://www.mydomain.com/phpMyAdmin';
```

Upgrading phpMyAdmin

New parameters appear in config.inc.php from version to version. If we do not wish to
modify their default values, we can reuse old configuration files, thus keeping the
defaults for the new parameters intact. Of course, if a new feature has a parameter that we
need to change, it might be easier to start over from the new file.

It is recommended to install the new version in a distinct directory, rename
config.inc.php to config.inc.new.php to keep it for reference, and copy our old
config.inc.php into this directory. We can then make the necessary adjustments (like
$cfg['PmaAbsoluteUri']) and test this new installation.

Special care must be taken to propagate the changes we might have made to the
layout.inc.php files, depending on the used themes. We may even have to copy our
custom themes subdirectories if we added our own themes to the structure.

Summary

This chapter explained:

- The common reasons for installing phpMyAdmin
- The steps for downloading it from the main site, basic configuration, and uploading to our web server
- Using a single copy of phpMyAdmin to manage multiple servers
- Using authentication types to fulfill the needs of a users' group while protecting data
- Securing our phpMyAdmin installation
- Upgrading phpMyAdmin

Interface Overview

Panels and Windows

The phpMyAdmin interface is composed of various panels and windows. Each panel has a specific function, and it's not possible to view all panels at the same time. We will first provide a quick overview of each panel, and then take a detailed look later in this chapter.

Login Panels

The login panel that appears depends on the authentication type chosen. For the http type, it will take the form of our browser's HTTP pop-up screen. For the cookie type, the phpMyAdmin-specific login panel will be displayed (covered in Chapter 2). By default, a Server choice dialog and a Language selector are present on this panel.

However, if we are using the config authentication type, no login panel is displayed, and the first displayed interface contains the left and right panels.

Left and Right Panels

These panels go together and are displayed during most part of our working session with phpMyAdmin. The **left panel** is our navigation guide through databases and tables. The **right panel** is the main working area where the data is managed and results appear. Its exact layout depends on the choices made from the left panel, and the sequence of operations performed.

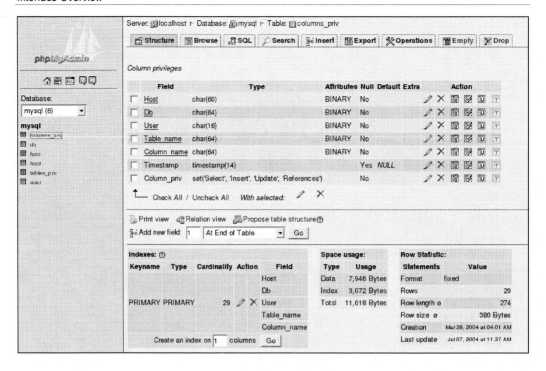

Home Page

The right panel can take the form of the Home page, which contains various links related to MySQL operations or phpMyAdmin information, a Language selector, and possibly the themes selector.

Views

In the right panel, we can choose the Database view, where we can take various actions about a specific database, or the Table view, where we can access many functions to manage a table. A system administrator can access the Server view as well. All these views have a top menu, which takes the form of tabs that lead to different sub-pages used to present information regrouped by common functions (table structure, privileges, etc.).

Query Window

This is a distinct window that can be opened from the left or the right panel. Its main purpose is to facilitate work on queries and see the results on the right panel.

Starting Page

When we start phpMyAdmin, we will see the following (depending on the authentication type specified in `config.inc.php`, and whether it has more than one server defined in it):

- One of the login panels
- The left and right panels, with the home page displayed on the right panel

Window Titles Configuration

When the left and right panels are displayed, the window's title changes to reflect *which* MySQL server, database, and table are active. phpMyAdmin also shows some information about the web server's host name if `$cfg['ShowHttpHostTitle']` is set to TRUE. What is displayed depends on another setting, `$cfg['SetHttpHostTitle']`. If this setting is empty (as it is by default), the true web server's host name appears in the title. We can put another string here, like 'my Web server', and this will be shown instead of the true host name.

Seeing the web server's host name can come in handy when we have many phpMyAdmin windows open, thus being connected to more than one *web* server. Of course, each phpMyAdmin window can itself give access to many *MySQL* servers.

General Icon Configuration

When various warning, error, or information messages are displayed, they can be accompanied by an icon, if `$cfg['ErrorIconic']` is set to TRUE. Another parameter, `$cfg['ReplaceHelpImg']`, when set to TRUE, displays a small icon containing a question mark at every place where documentation is available for a specific subject. These two parameters are set to TRUE by default, thus producing:

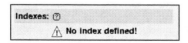

They can be independently set to FALSE. Setting both to FALSE would give:

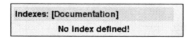

Natural Sort Order for Database and Table Names

Usually, computers sort items in lexical order, which gives the following results for a list of tables:

```
table1
table10
```

```
table2
table3
```

phpMyAdmin now implements 'natural sort order' by default, as specified by $cfg['NaturalOrder'] being TRUE. Thus, the database and table lists in left and right panels are sorted as:

```
table1
table2
table3
table10
```

Language Selection

A Language selector appears on the login panel (if any) and on the Home page. The default behavior of phpMyAdmin is to use the language defined in our browser's preferences, if there is a corresponding language file for this version.

The default language used in case the program cannot detect one is defined in config.inc.php in the $cfg['DefaultLang'] parameter with 'en-iso-8859-1'. This value can be changed. The possible values for language names are defined in the libraries/select_lang.lib.php script as an array.

Even if the default language is defined, each user (this is especially true on a multi-user installation) can choose his or her preferred language from the selector:

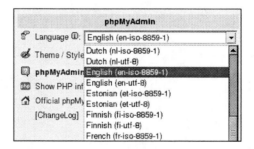

The user's choice will be remembered in a cookie whenever possible.

The small information icon beside Language gives access to phpMyAdmin's translator page, which lists, by language, the official translator and the contact information. This way we can reach the translator for corrections or to offer help on un-translated messages. We can also force a single language by setting the $cfg['Lang'] parameter with a value, such as 'en-iso-8859-1'.

On the Home page, we might be seeing also a MySQL Charset selector or MySQL Charset information (not in a selector). You can refer to Chapter 17, *Character Sets and Collations*, for full details on this subject.

Themes

A theme system is available in phpMyAdmin starting with version 2.6.0. The color parameters and the various icons are located in a structure under the themes subdirectory. For each available theme, there is a subdirectory named after the theme. It contains:

- layout.inc.php for the theme parameters
- css directory with the various CSS scripts
- img directory containing the icons
- screen.png, a screenshot of this theme

Theme Configuration

In config.inc.php, the $cfg['ThemePath'] parameter contains 'themes' by default, which indicates *which* subdirectory the needed structure is located in. This could be changed to point to another directory where our company's specific phpMyAdmin themes are located.

The default chosen theme is specified in $cfg['ThemeDefault'], and is set to 'original'. If no theme selection is available for users, this theme will be used.

> The original subdirectory should *never* be deleted; phpMyAdmin relies on it for normal operations.

Theme Selection

On the Home page, we can offer a theme selector to users. Setting $cfg['ThemeManager'] to TRUE (the default) shows the selector:

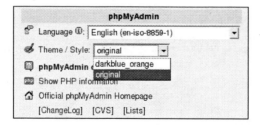

To help choose a suitable theme, the color palette icon next to Theme / Style brings us screenshots of the available themes. We can then click on take it under the theme we want. The chosen theme is remembered in a cookie.

Left Panel

The left panel contains the following elements:

- The logo (if $cfg['LeftDisplayLogo']$ is set to TRUE), which is clickable and linked to http://www.phpMyAdmin.net
- The server list (if $cfg['LeftDisplayServers'] = TRUE;)
- The Home link or icon (takes you back to the phpMyAdmin home page)
- A Log out link or icon
- A link or icon leading to the Query window
- Icons to display phpMyAdmin and MySQL documentation
- The databases and tables choices, with a statistic about the number of tables per database

If $cfg['MainPageIconic']$ is set to TRUE (the default), we see the *icons*. If it is set to FALSE, we see the Home, Log out, and Query window *links*.

The left panel can be resized by clicking and moving the vertical separation line in the preferred direction, to reveal more data in case the database or table names are too long for the default left panel size.

We can customize the appearance of this panel—all parameters are located in themes/themename/layout.inc.php except where noted otherwise. $cfg['LeftWidth']$ contains the default width of the left frame, in pixels. The background color is defined in $cfg['LeftBgColor']$ with a default value of '#D0DCE0'. The $cfg['LeftPointerColor']$ parameter, with a default value of '#CCFFCC', defines the pointer color (the pointer appears when we are using the Full mode, discussed shortly). To activate the left pointer for any theme being used, a master setting, $cfg['LeftPointerEnable']$, exists in config.inc.php. Its default value is TRUE.

Database and Table List

The following examples show that no database has been chosen from the drop-down menu:

It is also possible that we see the following screen:

This means that our current MySQL rights do not allow us to see any existing databases.

> A MySQL server always has *at least* one database (named mysql), but in this case, we do not have the right to see it.

We may have the right to create one, as explained in Chapter 4.

Light Mode

The left panel can have two forms: the Light mode or the Full mode. The Light mode is used by default, defined by a TRUE value in $cfg['LeftFrameLight']. The Light mode shows a drop-down list of the available databases, and only tables of the currently chosen database are displayed (here we have chosen the mysql database):

Clicking on the database name opens the right panel in the Database view, and clicking on a table name opens the right panel in the Table view (see the *Right Panel* section for details).

Table Short Statistics

Moving the cursor over a table name displays comments about the table (if any) and the number of rows currently in it:

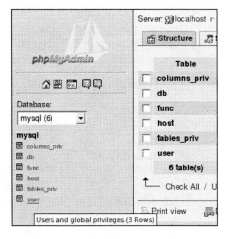

Quick-Browsing a Table

The small icon beside each table name is a quick way to browse the table's rows. It opens the right panel in Table view, browsing the first page of data from this table.

Full Mode

The previous examples were shown in Light mode, but setting the
$cfg['LeftFrameLight'] parameter to FALSE produces a complete layout of our
databases and tables, using collapsible menus (if supported by the browser):

The number of tables per database is shown in brackets. The Full mode is not selected by
default; it can increase network traffic and server load if our current rights give us access
to a large number of databases and tables. Links must be generated in the left panel to
enable table access and quick-browse access to every table, and the server has to count
the number of rows for all tables.

Nested Display of Tables Within a Database

MySQL's data structure is based on two levels: databases and tables. This does not allow
subdivisions of tables per project, a feature often requested by MySQL users. They must
rely on having multiple databases, but this is not always allowed by their provider. To
help them in this regard, phpMyAdmin introduces a **nested-levels** feature, based on the
table naming. This feature is currently available in Full mode only.

Let's say we have access to db1 database and two projects, marketing and payroll. Using a
special separator (by default a double underscore) between the project name and the table
name, we can achieve a visually interesting effect:

This feature is parameterized with $cfg['LeftFrameTableSeparator'] (set here to '__') to choose the characters that will mark each level change, and $cfg['LeftFrameTableLevel'] (set here to '1') for the number of sub-levels.

> The nested-level feature is only intended for improving the left panel look. The proper way to reference the tables in MySQL statements stays the same: for example, db1.payroll__jobs.

Beginning with phpMyAdmin 2.6.0, a click in the left panel *on the project name* (here payroll) opens this project in the right panel, showing only those project's tables.

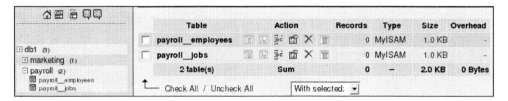

Server-List Choice

If we have to manage multiple servers from the same phpMyAdmin window and need to often switch between servers, it might prove useful to always see the list of servers in the left frame:

For this, the $cfg['LeftDisplayServers'] parameter must be set to TRUE. The list of servers can have two forms: dropdowns or links. Which form appears depends on $cfg['DisplayServersList']. By default, this parameter is set to FALSE, so we see a drop-down list of servers. Setting $cfg['DisplayServersList'] to TRUE produces a links-style list:

Right Panel

The right panel is the main working area, and all the possible views for it are explained in the following sections. Its appearance can be customized. The background color is defined in $cfg['RightBgColor'], and the default color is #F5F5F5. We can also put a background image by setting the URI of the image we want (for example, http://www.domain.com/images/clouds.jpg) in $cfg['RightBgImage'].

Home Page

The home page may contain a varying number of links, depending on the login mode and the user's rights. A normal user may see it as:

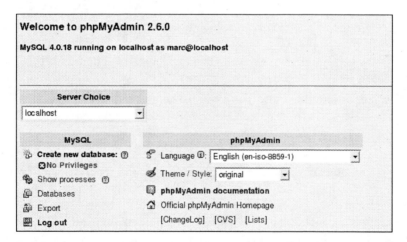

The Home link from the left panel is used to display this page. It shows the phpMyAdmin and MySQL version, the MySQL server name, and the logged-in user. We also see that this user does not have the privilege to create a database. We see some links that relate to MySQL or phpMyAdmin itself. The Log out link might not be there if automatic login was done, as indicated by the configuration file.

In this example, a normal user is not allowed to change his or her password from the interface. To allow this password change, we set $cfg['ShowChgPassword'] to TRUE. Privileged users have more options on the home page. They can always create databases, and have more links to manage the server as a whole (Server view):

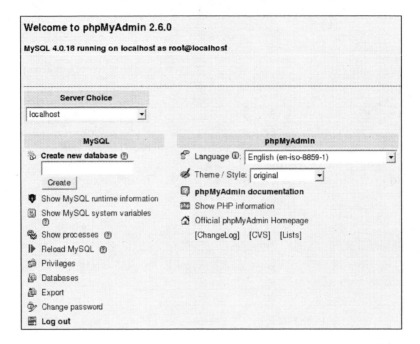

Database View

phpMyAdmin goes into this view (shown in the screenshot that follows) every time we click on a database name from the left frame, or if the USE command followed by a database name is typed in a SQL box.

This is where we can see an overview of the database: the existing tables, a link to create a table, the tabs to the Database view sub-pages, and some special operations we might do on this database to generate documentation and statistics. There is a checkbox beside each table to make global operations on those tables (covered in Chapter 10). The table is chosen by using the checkbox or by clicking anywhere on the row's background. We can also see each table's size, if $cfg['ShowStats'] is set to TRUE. This parameter also controls the display of table-specific statistics in the Table view.

In this screen, we currently see an error message. We can safely ignore it for now, because in the *Relational System* section (Chapter 11) we will carry out the initial setup for special linked-tables features.

The initial screen that appears here is the database Structure sub-page. We might want a different initial sub-page to appear when entering the Database view. This is controlled by the $cfg['DefaultTabDatabase']$ parameter, and the available choices are given in the configuration file as comments.

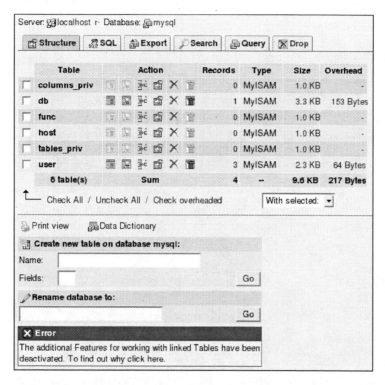

The number of records is obtained using a quick method—*not* by doing a SELECT COUNT(*) FROM TABLENAME. This quick method is usually accurate, except for InnoDB tables, which returns an approximate number of records. To help get the correct number of records, even for InnoDB, the $cfg['MaxExactCount']$ parameter is available. If the approximate number of records is lower than this parameter's value—by default, 20000—the slower SELECT COUNT(*) method will be used.

> Do *not* put a value too high for this parameter. You would get correct results, but only after waiting for a few minutes, if there are hundreds of thousands of records in your InnoDB table.

Table View

This is a commonly used view, giving access to all table-specific sub-pages. Usually, the initial screen is the table's Structure screen, which shows (note the upper part) all fields and indexes. Note that the header for this screen always shows the current database and table names. We also see the comments set for the table:

41

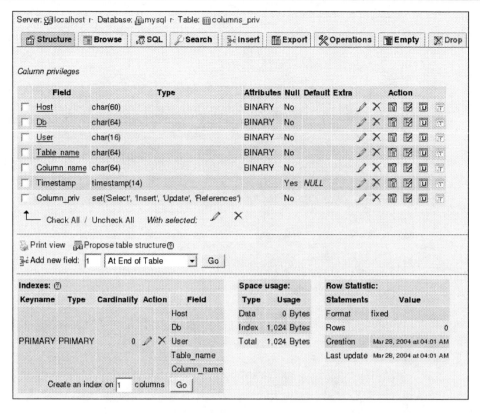

The lower part of the Structure page enables us to run queries and insert data from an external source file. All these functions will be discussed in subsequent chapters.

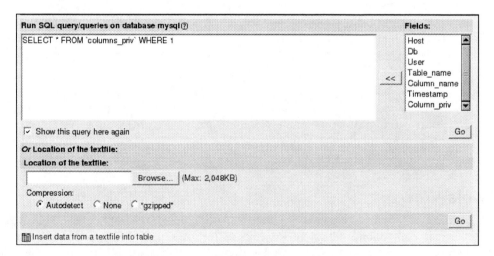

The $cfg['DefaultTabTable']$ parameter defines the initial sub-page on the Table view. Some users prefer to avoid seeing the structure, because in production they routinely run saved queries or enter the Search sub-page (explained in Chapter 9).

Server View

This view is entered each time we choose a MySQL-related option from the Home page: for example, Databases or Show MySQL runtime information. A privileged user will of course see more choices in the Server view. The Server view panel was created to group together related server management sub-pages and enable easy navigation between them.

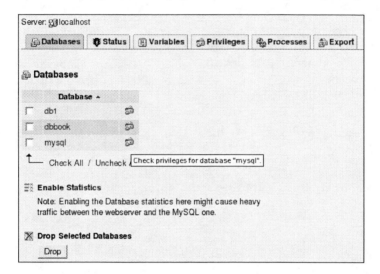

The default Server page is controlled by the $cfg['DefaultTabServer']$ parameter. This parameter defines the initial starting page as well. For multi-user installations, it is recommended to keep the default value (main.php), which displays the traditional home page. We could choose to display server statistics instead by changing this parameter to server_status.php, or to see the users list with server_privileges.php. Other possible choices are explained in the configuration file, and the server administration pages are explained in Chapter 18.

Icons for Home Page and Menu Tabs

A configuration parameter, $cfg['MainPageIconic']$, controls the appearance of icons at various places on the right panel:

- On the home page
- At top of page, when listing the Server, Database, and Table information
- On the menu tabs in Database, Table, and Server views

This parameter is set to TRUE by default, producing, for example:

Query Window

It is often convenient to have a *distinct window* in which we can type and refine queries, and which is synchronized with the right panel. This window is called the Query window. We can open this window by using the small SQL icon or the Query window link from the left panel's icons or links zone.

This link or icon are displayed if $cfg['QueryFrame'] is set to TRUE. The TRUE for $cfg['QueryFrameJS'] tells phpMyAdmin to open a distinct window and update it using JavaScript commands; of course, this only works for a JavaScript-enabled browser. If this is set to FALSE, clicking on Query window will only open the right panel and will display the normal SQL sub-page.

> The full usability of the Query window is only achieved with the distinct window mode.

The Query window itself has sub-pages and it appears here over the right panel:

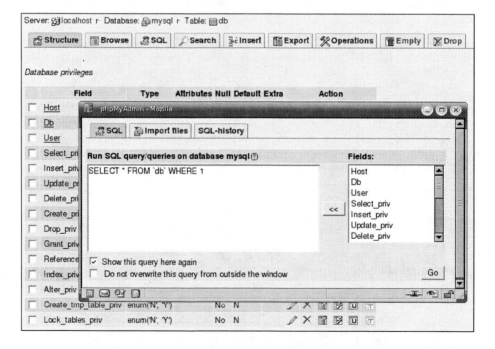

We can choose the dimensions (in pixels) of this window with
`$cfg['QueryWindowWidth']` and `$cfg['QueryWindowHeight']`. Chapter 12 explains the
Query window in more details, including the available SQL query history features.

Site-Specific Header and Footer

Some users may want to display a company logo, a link to the helpdesk, or other
information on the phpMyAdmin interface. In the main phpMyAdmin directory, two
scripts—`config.header.inc.php` and `config.footer.inc.php`—are available for this
purpose. We can add our own PHP or XHTML code in these scripts, and it will appear at
the beginning (for header) or end of page (for footer):

- On the cookie login page
- On the right panel

MySQL Documentation Links

phpMyAdmin displays links to the MySQL documentation, at various places on its
interface. These links refer to the exact point in the official MySQL documentation to
learn about a MySQL command. We can customize the location, language, and manual
type referred to, with the following configuration parameters:

```
$cfg['MySQLManualBase'] = 'http://www.mysql.com/doc/en';
$cfg['MySQLManualType'] = 'searchable';
```

You may take a look at `http://www.mysql.com/documentation` to see the languages in
which the manual is available, and change the parameters accordingly. For the manual
type, the most up-to-date possible values are explained as comments in `config.inc.php`.
Users who prefer to keep a copy of this documentation on a local server would specify a
local link here.

The `$cfg['ReplaceHelpImg']` parameter controls how the links are displayed. Its
default value of TRUE makes phpMyAdmin display small question-mark icons, and FALSE
shows Documentation links.

Summary

In this chapter we have covered:

- The language selection system
- The purpose of the left and right panels
- The contents of the left panel, including Light mode and Full mode

- The contents of the right panel, with its various views, depending on the context
- The Query window
- Customization of MySQL documentation links

First Steps

Database Creation

Having seen the overall layout of phpMyAdmin's panel, we are ready to create a database and our first table, insert some data in it, and browse it. Before creating a table, we must ensure that we have a database for which the MySQL server's administrator has given us the CREATE privilege. Various possibilities exist:

- The administrator has already created a database for us, and we see its name in the left panel; we don't have the right to create an additional database.

- We have the right to create databases from phpMyAdmin.

- We are on a shared host and the host provider has installed a general Web interface (for example, Cpanel) to create MySQL databases and accounts.

No Privileges?

In this case, the Home page looks like the following screenshot:

This means that we must work with the databases already created for us, or ask the MySQL server's administrator to give us the necessary CREATE privilege.

In case you *are* the MySQL server's administrator, please refer to Chapter 18, *MySQL Server Administration with phpMyAdmin*.

First Database Creation Is Authorized

If phpMyAdmin detects that we have the right to create a database, the home page looks as shown in the following figure:

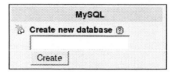

If we are restricted to the use of a prefix, the prefix might be suggested in the input field (a popular choice for this prefix is the username).

We will assume here that we have the right to create a database named dbbook. We enter dbbook in the input field and click on Create. Once the database is created, we will see the following screen:

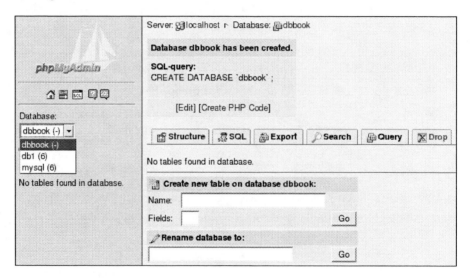

Notice the following:

- The main title of the right panel has changed to reflect the fact that we are now located in this database.

- A confirmation message regarding the creation is displayed.

- The left panel has been updated; we see dbbook (-). Here, the name indicates that the dbbook database has been created, and the - symbol indicates that it contains no tables.

- By default, the SQL query sent to the server by phpMyAdmin to create the database is displayed in color.

phpMyAdmin displays the query it generated, because $cfg['ShowSQL'] is set to TRUE. Looking at the generated queries can be a good way of learning SQL.

It is important to examine the phpMyAdmin feedback to ascertain the validity of the operations we make through the interface. This way, we can detect errors like typos in the names or creation of a table in the wrong database.

Database Renaming

Starting with phpMyAdmin 2.6.0, a Rename database dialog is shown in the Database view. Although this operation is not directly supported by MySQL, phpMyAdmin does it indirectly by creating a new database, renaming each table—thus sending it to the new database—and finally dropping the original database.

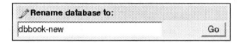

Creating Our First Table

Now that we have a new database, it's time to create a table in it. The example table we will use is the familiar books table.

Choosing the Fields

Before creating a table, we should plan the information we want to store. This is usually done using database design, entity-relationship diagramming, and table normalization. In our case, a simple analysis leads us to the following book-related data we want to keep:

- International Standard Book Number (ISBN)
- Book title
- Number of pages
- Author identification

For now, it is not important to have the complete list of fields (or columns) for our books table; we will modify it by prototyping the application and refine it later. At end of the chapter, we will add a second table, authors, containing information about each author.

Table Creation

We have chosen our table name and we know the number of fields. We enter this information in the Create new table dialog and click Go to start creating the table:

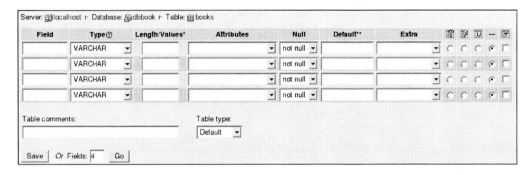

We then see a panel to specify field information. Since we asked for four fields, we get four rows, each row referring to information specific to one field:

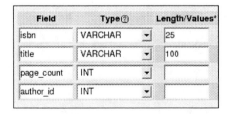

Another column, Collation, might be shown at this point. Please refer to Chapter 17, *Character Sets and Collations*.

The MySQL documentation explains valid characters for table and field names (if we search for Legal names). This may vary depending on the MySQL version. Usually, any character that is allowed in a file name (except the dot and the slash) is acceptable in a table name, and the length of the name must not exceed 64 characters. The 64-character limit exists for field names as well; however, we can use any character.

We enter our field names under the Field column. Each field has a type, the VARCHAR type (variable character) being the default since it is commonly used. The VARCHAR type is widely used when the field content is alphanumeric, because the contents will occupy only the space needed for it. This type requires a maximum length, which we specify. If we forget to do so, a small pop-up message reminds us later when we save. For the page count and the author identification, we have chosen INT type (integer), as depicted in the following screenshot:

Field	Type⑦	Length/Values*
isbn	VARCHAR	25
title	VARCHAR	100
page_count	INT	
author_id	INT	

There are other attributes for fields, but we will leave them empty in this short example. You might notice the Fields: 4 dialog at the bottom of the screen. This is not just a reminder of the number of fields we asked for. In fact, we can use it to change the number of fields we want (usually increasing it), and hit Go. The number of rows would change according to the new number of fields, *leaving intact the information already entered* about the four first fields. Before saving the page, let's define some keys.

Choosing Keys

A table should normally have a primary key (a field with unique content that represents each row). Having a primary key is recommended for row identification, better performance, and possible cross-table relations. A good value here is the ISBN, so we select Primary for the isbn field. As $cfg['PropertiesIconic'] is set to TRUE by default, we see icons indicating the various index possibilities. Moving the mouse over them or over the radio buttons reveals Primary, Index, Unique, and Full text.

> Index (also referred to as **Key**) management can be done at initial table creation, or later in the Structure sub-page of Table view.

To improve the speed of queries we will make by author ID, we should add an index on this field. Our screen now looks like this:

Field	Type⑦	Length/Values*	Attributes	Null	Default**	Extra						
isbn	VARCHAR	25		not null					Primary			
title	VARCHAR	100		not null								
page_count	INT			not null								
author_id	INT			not null								

At this point, we could change the table type using the Type drop-down menu, but for now we will just accept the default type.

Now we are ready to create the table by clicking on Save. If all goes well, the next screen confirms that the table has been created; we are now in the Structure sub-page of Table view.

If we forget to specify a value in the Length column for a CHAR or VARCHAR, phpMyAdmin would remind us before trying to create the table.

Of the various tabs leading to other sub-pages, some are not active because it would not make sense to browse or search a table if there are no rows in it. It would, however, be acceptable to export, because we can export a table's structure even if it contains no data.

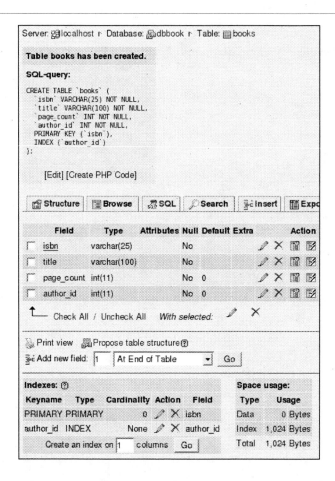

Manual Data Insertion

Now that we have a table, let's put some data in it manually. Before doing so, here are some useful references on data manipulation within this book:

- Chapter 5 explains how to change data.

- Chapter 8 explains how to import data from existing files.

- Chapter 10 explains how to copy data from other tables.

- Chapter 11 explains the relational system (in our case, we will want to link to the authors table).

For now, click on the Insert link, which will lead us to the data-entry (or edit) panel (shown in the screenshot that follows).

We can enter the following sample information for two books:

- ISBN: 1-234567-89-0, title: A hundred years of cinema (volume 1), 600 pages, author ID: 1

- ISBN: 1-234567-22-0, title: Future souvenirs, 200 pages, author ID: 2

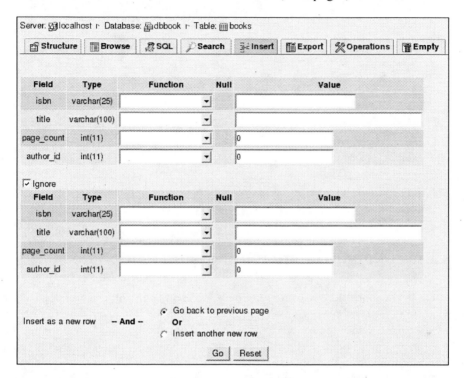

This screen has room to enter information for two rows—two books. This is because the default value of $cfg['InsertRows'] is 2. By default, the Ignore checkbox is ticked, which means that the second group of fields will be ignored. But as soon as we enter some information in one field of this group and exit the field, the Ignore box is unchecked.

We start by entering data for the first and second rows. The Value column width obeys the maximum length for the character fields. If we want to enter data for more books after these two, we select Insert another new row. We then click on Go to insert data:

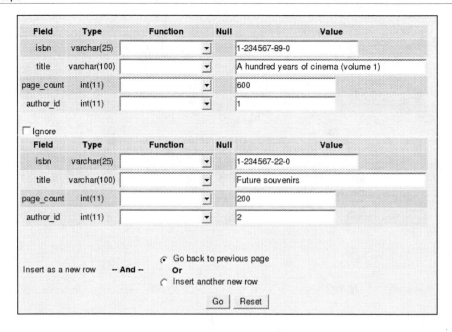

Data Entry Panel Tuning for chars and varchars

By default, phpMyAdmin displays an input field on a single line for field types CHAR and VARCHAR. This is controlled by setting $cfg['CharEditing'] to 'input'. Sometimes we may want to insert line breaks (new lines) within the field (this insertion might be done manually with the *Enter* key, or while copying and pasting lines of text from another on-screen source). This is possible by changing $cfg['CharEditing'] to 'textarea'. This is a global setting and will apply to all fields of all tables, for all users of this copy of phpMyAdmin.

We can tune the number of columns and rows of this text area with:

```
$cfg['CharTextareaCols']   = 40;
$cfg['CharTextareaRows']   = 2;
```

Here, 2 for $cfg['CharTextareaRows'] means that we should be able to see at least two lines before the browser starts to display a vertical scroll bar. These settings apply to all CHAR and VARCHAR fields, and using them would generate a different Insert screen as follows:

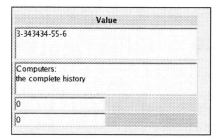

With this entry mode, the maximum length of each field no longer applies visually, but would be enforced by MySQL at INSERT time.

Browse Mode

There are many ways to enter this mode. In fact, it is used each time query results are displayed. We can enter this mode manually using the quick-browse icon on the left panel, or by going to Table view for a specific table and clicking Browse:

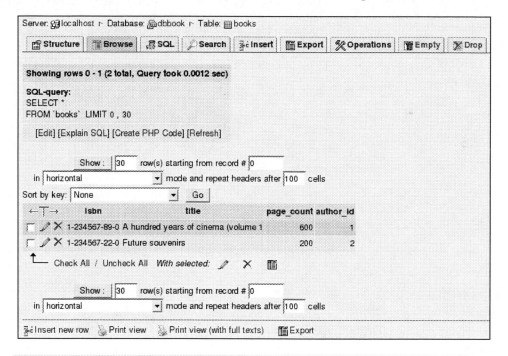

The checkboxes beside each row of results and the With selected menu will be explained in Chapter 5.

SQL Query Links

In the Browse results, the first part displayed is the query itself, along with a few links. The displayed links may vary depending on our actions and some configuration parameters:

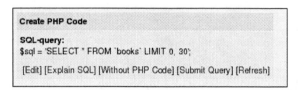

The Edit link appears if $cfg['SQLQuery']['Edit'] is set to TRUE. Its purpose is to open the Query window, to be able to edit this query (see Chapter 12, *Entering SQL Commands*).

Explain SQL is displayed if $cfg['SQLQuery']['Explain'] is set to TRUE. We will see in Chapter 6, *Changing Table Structure*, what this link can be used for.

The Create PHP Code link can be clicked to reformat the query to the syntax expected in a PHP script. It can then be copied and pasted directly at the place where we need the query, in the PHP script we are working on. Note that after a click this link changes to Without PHP Code, which would bring back the normal query display. This link is available if $cfg['SQLQuery']['ShowAsPHP'] is set to TRUE:

Create PHP Code

SQL-query:
$sql = 'SELECT * FROM `books` LIMIT 0, 30';

[Edit] [Explain SQL] [Without PHP Code] [Submit Query] [Refresh]

Refresh is used to execute the same query again. The results might change, since a MySQL server is a multi-user server, and other users might be modifying the same table(s). This link is shown if $cfg['SQLQuery']['Refresh'] is set to TRUE.

All these four parameters have a default value of TRUE in config.inc.php.

Navigation Bar

This bar is displayed at the top of results and also at the bottom. Column headers can be repeated at certain intervals among results, depending on the value entered in repeat headers after....

In the previous example, the bar was simple:

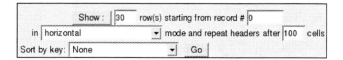

The bar enables us to navigate from page to page, displaying an arbitrary number of records (or rows), starting at some point in the results. Since we entered browse mode by clicking Browse, the underlying query that generated the results includes the whole table. However, this is not always the case.

Notice that we are positioned at record number 0, and are seeing records in horizontal mode.

Let's take another example, this time with a newly introduced table—the student-course table. This table contains three fields: the student ID (referring to a student table), the course ID (from a course table), and the date when this student ends this course. As this table has many rows (here 32109), the navigation bar adapts itself:

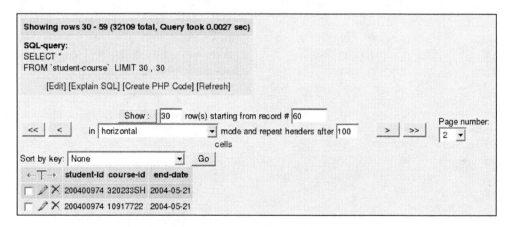

This time, there are buttons labeled <<, <, >, and >> for easy access to the first page, previous page, next page, and the last page of the results. These symbols are displayed in this manner because the default setting of $cfg['NavigationBarIconic']$ is TRUE. A FALSE here would produce a different set of labels:

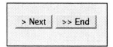

There is also a Page number drop-down menu, to directly go to one of the pages located near the current page. Since there can be hundreds or thousands of pages, this menu is kept small, with only a few page numbers before and after the current page. Selecting vertical mode on the student-course table generates the following screen:

Showing rows 95 - 99 (32109 total, Query took 0.0027 sec)

SQL-query:
SELECT *
FROM `student-course` LIMIT 95 , 5

   [Edit] [Explain SQL] [Create PHP Code] [Refresh]

Show : 5 row(s) starting from record # 100
<< < in vertical ▾ mode and repeat headers after 100 > >> Page number: 20 ▾
cells

Sort by key: None ▾ Go

←T→

student-Id	200281762	200281762	200279812	200275716	200268636
course-Id	152513SH	152294SH	2022A3RE	60110204	10913811
end-date	2004-05-21	2004-05-21	2004-05-21	2004-05-21	2004-05-21

Check All / Uncheck All   With selected: ✎   ✕   📋

By design, phpMyAdmin always tries to give quick results, and one way to achieve this result is by adding a LIMIT clause in SELECT. If there is already a LIMIT clause in the original query, phpMyAdmin will respect it. The default limit is 30 rows, set in $cfg['MaxRows']. With multiple users on the server, this helps keeping the server load to a minimum.

Another button is available on the navigation bar, but must be activated by setting $cfg['ShowAll'] to TRUE. It would be very tempting for users to use this button often. So, on a multi-user installation of phpMyAdmin, it is recommended that it be disabled (FALSE). When enabled, the navigation bar is augmented as shown:

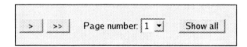

Clicking on the Show all button retrieves all the rows of the current results set, which might hit the execution time limit in PHP, or a memory limit in the server or browser.

If we enter a big number in the Show...rows dialog, the same results will be achieved (and we may face the same potential problems).

Sorting Results

In SQL, we can never be sure of the order in which the data is retrieved, unless we explicitly sort the data. Some implementations of the retrieving engine may show results in the same order as when data was entered, or by primary key, but a sure way to get results in the order we want is by sorting them explicitly.

One obvious way to sort is by key. The Sort dialog shows all the keys already defined. Here we see a key named PRIMARY, the name given to our primary key on the isbn field when we checked Primary for this field at creation time:

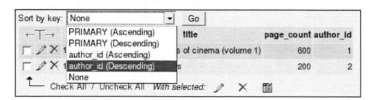

This might be the only way to sort on multiple fields at once (for multi-fields indexes).

If we choose to sort by author_id (Descending), we see:

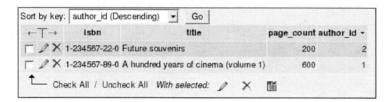

We now see a small red triangle pointing downwards beside the author_id header. This means that the current sort order is 'descending'. Moving the mouse cursor over the author_id header makes the red triangle change direction, to indicate what will happen if we click on the header: a sort by ascending author_id.

In fact, all the column headers can be clicked to sort on this column, even if they are not part of an index. We can confirm this by watching the SQL query at top of screen; it should contain an ORDER BY clause.

The default initial sort order is defined in $cfg['Order'] with ASC for ascending, DESC for descending, and SMART, which means that fields of type DATE, TIME, DATETIME, and TIMESTAMP would be sorted in descending order, and other field types in ascending order.

Color-Marking Rows

When moving the mouse between rows, the row background color may change to the color defined in $cfg['BrowsePointerColor']. This parameter can be found in themes/themename/layout.inc.php . To enable this browse pointer for all themes, $cfg['BrowsePointerEnable'] must be set to TRUE (the default) in config.inc.php.

It may be interesting to visually mark some rows to highlight their importance for personal comparison of data, or when showing data to people. Highlighting is done by clicking the row. Clicking again removes the mark on the row. The chosen color is defined by $cfg['BrowseMarkerColor'] (see themes/themename/layout.inc.php). This feature must be enabled by setting $cfg['BrowseMarkerEnable'] to TRUE, this time in config.inc.php—this sets the feature for all themes. We can mark more than one row. Marking the row also activates the checkbox for this row:

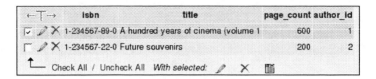

Limiting the Length of Each Column

In the previous examples, we always saw the full contents of each column, because their number of characters was within the limit defined by $cfg['LimitChars']. This is a limit enforced on all non-numeric fields. If this limit was lower (say 10), the display would be as follows:

This would help us see more columns at the same time (at the expense of seeing less of each column).

To reveal the full texts, we can click the T besides the column header, which toggles between the full-text mode and the partial-text mode:

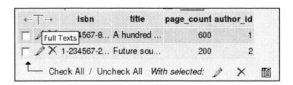

Browse-Mode Customization

Here are more parameters that control the appearance of results. These parameters—except $cfg['RepeatCells']—are located in themes/themename/layout.inc.php.

- $cfg['Border']: The HTML tables used to present results have no border by default because this parameter is set to 0; we can put a higher number (for example 1 or 2) to add borders to the tables.

$cfg['ThBgcolor']$: The mentioned tables have headers with #D3DCE3 as the default background color.

- $cfg['BgcolorOne']$, $cfg['BgcolorTwo']$: When displaying rows of results, two background colors are used alternately; by default, those are #CCCCCC and #DDDDDD.

- $cfg['RepeatCells']$: When many rows of data are displayed, we may lose track of the meaning of each column; by default, at each 100th cell, column headers are displayed.

Create an Additional Table

In our (simple) design, we know that we need another table: the authors table. The authors table will contain:

- Author identification
- Author's full name
- Phone number

To create this table, we must go back to Database view. In the left panel, we click on dbbook, and request the creation of another table with three fields:

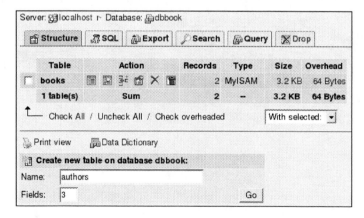

Using the same techniques used when creating the first table, we get:

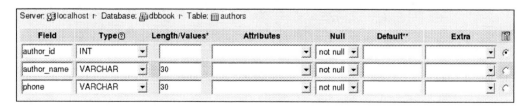

Here we use the same field name (author_id, which is our primary key in this new table), in order to be more consistent in our design. After saving the table structure, we enter some data for authors 1 and 2. Use your imagination for this!

Summary

In this chapter, we:

- Explained how to create a database and some tables
- Saw how to enter data manually in the tables
- Confirmed the presence of data by becoming familiar with browse mode, including the SQL query links, navigation bar, sorting options and row marking

5

Changing Data

Data is not static; it often changes. This chapter focuses on editing and deleting data and its supporting structures: tables and databases.

Edit Mode

When we browse a table or view results from a search on any single-table query, small icons appear at the left or right of each table row:

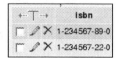

The row can be edited with the pencil-shaped icon, and deleted with the X-shaped icon. The exact form and location of these controls are governed by:

```
$cfg['PropertiesIconic']    = TRUE;
$cfg['ModifyDeleteAtLeft']  = TRUE;
$cfg['ModifyDeleteAtRight'] = FALSE;
```

We can decide whether to display them on the left, right, or both sides. The $cfg['PropertiesIconic'] parameter can have the values TRUE, FALSE, or 'both'. TRUE displays icons as seen in the previous image, FALSE displays Edit and Delete (or their translated equivalent) as links, and 'both' displays the icon *and* the text.

The small checkbox beside each row is explained in the *Multi-Row Edit* and the *Deleting Many Rows* sections later in this chapter.

Clicking on the Edit icon or link brings the following panel, similar to the data entry panel (except for the lower part):

Field	Type	Function	Null	Value
isbn	varchar(25)	▾		1-234567-89-0
title	varchar(100)	▾		A hundred years of cinema (volume 1)
page_count	int(11)	▾		600
author_id	int(11)	▾		1

⊙ Save
Or
○ Insert as a new row
   – And –

⊙ Go back to previous page
Or
○ Insert another new row
Or
○ Go back to this page

Go   Reset

In this panel, we can change data by direct typing (or cut and paste via the normal operating system mechanisms). We can also revert to the original contents using the Reset button.

By default, the lower radio buttons are set to Save (meaning we make changes to *this* row) and Go back to previous page (so that we can continue editing another row on the previous results page). We might want to stay on the current page after clicking Go—we want to save and to continue editing—so we can choose Go back to this page. If we want to insert yet another new row after saving the current row, we just have to choose Insert another new row before saving. The Insert as a new row choice is explained in the section *Duplicating Rows of Data* of this chapter.

Tab to Next Field

People who prefer to use the keyboard can use the *Tab* key to go to the next field. Normally, the cursor goes from left to right, top to bottom, and so it would travel into the fields in the Function column (more on this in a moment). However, to ease data navigation in phpMyAdmin, the normal order of navigation has been altered; the *Tab* key first goes through each field in the Value column, and then through each one in the Function column.

Handling of NULL Values

If the table's structure permits a NULL value inside a field, a small checkbox appears in the field's Null column. Checking it puts a NULL value in the field. A special mechanism has also been added to phpMyAdmin to ensure that if data is typed in the Value column for this field, the Null checkbox is cleared automatically (this is possible in JavaScript-enabled browsers).

Here, we have modified the structure (as explained in Chapter 6) of the phone field in the authors table to permit a NULL value. The Null checkbox is not checked here:

Field	Type	Function	Null	Value
author_id	int(11)	▾		1
author_name	varchar(30)	▾		John Smith
phone	varchar(30)	▾	☐	+01 445 789-1234

The data is erased after checking the Null box, as shown in the following screenshot:

Field	Type	Function	Null	Value
author_id	int(11)	▾		1
author_name	varchar(30)	▾		John Smith
phone	varchar(30)	▾	☑	

The Edit panel will appear this way if this row is ever brought on-screen again.

Applying a Function to a Value

The MySQL language offers some functions that we may apply to data before saving, and some of these functions appear in a drop-down menu, beside each field, if $cfg['ShowFunctionFields'] is set to TRUE.

The function list is defined in the $cfg['Functions'] array. The most commonly used functions for a certain data type are displayed first in the list. Some restrictions are defined in the $cfg['RestrictColumnTypes'] and $cfg['RestrictFunctions'] arrays to control *which* functions are displayed first.

Here are the definitions that restrict the function names to be displayed for the VARCHAR type:

```
$cfg['RestrictColumnTypes'] = array(
     'VARCHAR'        => 'FUNC_CHAR',  [...]

$cfg['RestrictFunctions'] = array(
     'FUNC_CHAR'      => array(
          'ASCII',
          'CHAR',
          'SOUNDEX',
          'LCASE',
          'UCASE',
          'PASSWORD',
          'MD5',
          'ENCRYPT',
          'LAST_INSERT_ID',
          'USER',
          'CONCAT'
     ),  [...]
```

As depicted in the following screenshot, we apply the UCASE function to the title when saving *this row*:

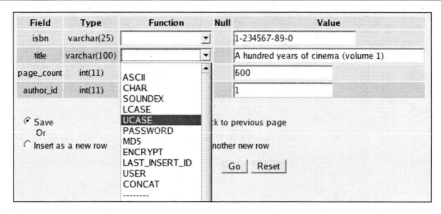

This feature may be disabled by setting $cfg['ShowFunctionFields']$ to FALSE to gain some screen space (to be able to see more of the data).

Duplicating Rows of Data

During the course of data maintenance (for permanent duplication or for test purposes), we often have to generate a copy of a row. If this is done in the same table, we must respect the rules of key uniqueness.

An example is in order here. Our author has written Volume 2 of his book about cinema, and the only fields that need a slight change are the ISBN number and the title. We bring the existing row on-screen, change these two fields, and choose Insert as a new row, as shown in the following screenshot:

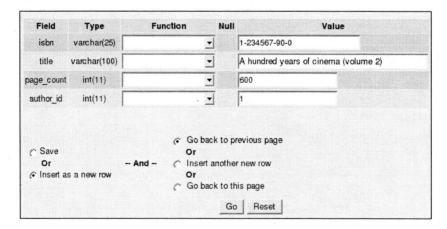

When we click Go, another row is created with the modified information, leaving the original row unchanged:

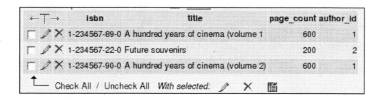

Multi-Row Edit

Starting with phpMyAdmin 2.5.5, the multi-row edit feature enables us to use checkboxes on the rows we want to edit, and use the Edit link (or the pencil-shaped icon) in the With selected menu. The Check All / Uncheck All links can also be used to quickly check or uncheck all the boxes. We can also click anywhere on the row's data to activate the corresponding checkbox.

This brings up an Edit panel containing all the chosen rows, and the editing process may continue while the data from these rows is seen, compared, and changed.

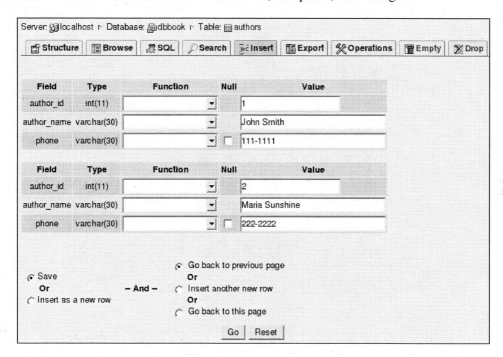

When we mark some rows with the checkboxes, we can also perform two other actions on them: delete (see the *Deleting Many Rows* section in this chapter) and export (see Chapter 7).

Deleting Data

phpMyAdmin's interface enables us to delete the following:

- Single rows of data
- Multiple rows of a table
- All rows of a table
- All rows of multiple tables

Deleting Single Rows

We can use the small X-shaped icon beside each row to delete the row. If the value of $cfg['Confirm'] is set to TRUE, every MySQL DELETE statement has to be confirmed before execution. This behavior is default; it might prove not prudent to be able to delete a row with just one click!

The form of the confirmation itself varies depending on the browser's ability to execute JavaScript. A JavaScript-based confirmation popup would look like the following screenshot:

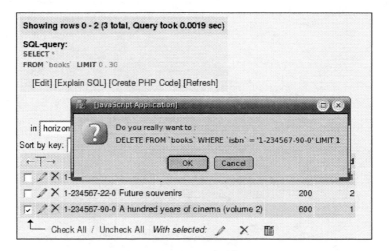

If JavaScript has been disabled, a distinct panel appears:

The actual DELETE statement will use whatever information is best to ensure the deletion of only the intended row. In our case, a primary key had been defined, and was used in the WHERE clause. In the absence of a primary key, a longer WHERE clause will be generated based on the value of each field. The WHERE clause might even prevent the correct execution of the DELETE operation, especially if there are TEXT or BLOB fields, because the HTTP transaction used to send the query to the web server may be limited in length by the browser or the server.

Deleting Many Rows

A feature added to phpMyAdmin in version 2.5.4 is the multi-row delete. Let's say we examine a page of rows and decide that some rows have to be destroyed. Instead of deleting them one by one with the Delete link or icon—and because sometimes the decision to delete must be made while examining a group of rows—there are checkboxes beside rows in Table view mode:

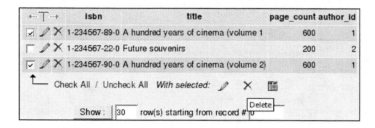

These are used with the With selected X-shaped icon. A confirmation screen appears, listing all the rows that are about to be deleted. It is also possible to click anywhere on the row's data to activate the corresponding checkbox.

Deleting All Rows of a Table

To completely erase all rows of a table (leaving its structure intact), we go to the Database view and click on the database name in the left panel. We then click on the trash can icon located on the same line as the table we want to empty:

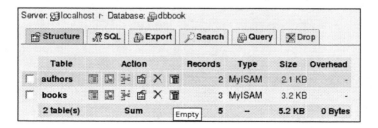

We get a message confirming the TRUNCATE (the MySQL statement used to quickly empty a table). Emptying a table can also be done in Table view, with the Empty link located on the top menu:

Deleting data, either row-by-row or by emptying a table, is a permanent action. No recovery is possible except with our backups.

Deleting All Rows of Many Tables

The screen before last shows a checkbox to the left of each table name. We can choose some tables, then in the With selected menu, choose the Empty operation as shown in the following screen:

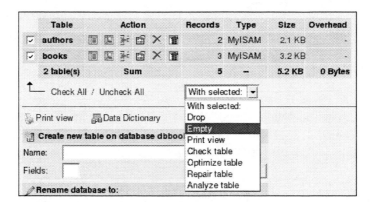

Of course, this decision must not be taken lightly!

Deleting Tables

Deleting a table erases the data *and* the table's structure. We can delete tables using the Drop link in Table view:

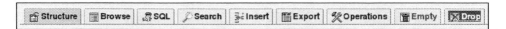

In Database view, we could delete a specific table by using the X-shaped icon for that table. The same mechanism also exists for deleting more that one table (with the drop-down menu and the Drop action).

The Empty and Drop actions are marked in red to better indicate the inherent danger of these actions on data.

Deleting Databases

We can delete a whole database—including all its tables—using the Drop link in Database view:

By default, $cfg['AllowUserDropDatabase'] is set to FALSE, so this link is hidden to unprivileged users until this setting is manually changed to TRUE.

To help us think twice, a special message appears before a database is deleted: You are about to DESTROY a complete database!

Summary

In this chapter, we examined the following concepts:

- Editing data, including the null field and using the *Tab* key
- Applying a function to a value
- Duplicating rows of data
- Deleting data, tables, and databases

6

Changing Table Structure

This chapter explores editing table definitions and using special column types. When developing an application, requirements often change because of new or modified needs. Developers must accommodate these changes through judicious table-structure editing.

Adding a Field

Suppose we need a new field to store a book's language, and by default, the books on which we keep data are written in English. We decide that the field will be called language, and will be a code composed of two characters (en by default).

In the Structure sub-page of the Table view for the books table, we can find the Add new field dialog. Here, we specify how many new fields we want and where the new fields go.

The positions of the new fields in the table only matter from a developer's point of view; we usually group the fields logically to find them more easily in the list of fields. The exact position of the fields will not play a role in the intended results (output from the queries), because these results can be adjusted regardless of the table structure. Usually, the most important fields (including the keys) are located at the beginning of the table, but this is a matter of personal preference.

We choose to put the new field At End of Table, so we check the corresponding radio button and click on Go:

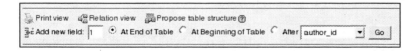

Other possible choices would be At Beginning of Table and After -- (where we would have to choose from the drop-down menu the field after which the new field must go).

We see the familiar panel for the new fields, repeated for the number of fields asked for. We fill it, and this time we put a default value, en. We then click on Save.

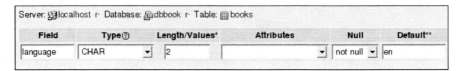

This panel appeared in horizontal mode, the default for $cfg['DefaultPropDisplay'].

Vertical Mode

If we set $cfg['DefaultPropDisplay'] to 'vertical', the panel to add new fields (along with the panel to edit a field's structure) will be presented in vertical order. The advantages of working in vertical mode become obvious especially when there are more choices for each field, as explained in Chapter 16, *MIME-Based Transformations*.

Let's see how the panel appears if we are in vertical mode and ask for three new fields:

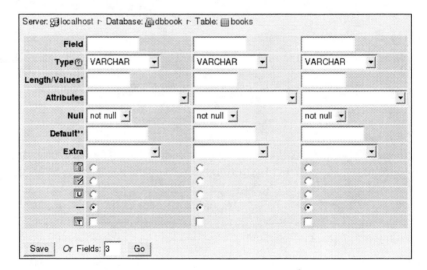

Editing Field Attributes

On the Structure sub-page, we can make further changes to our table. For this example, we have set $cfg['PropertiesIconic'] to 'both' to see the icons along with their text explanation:

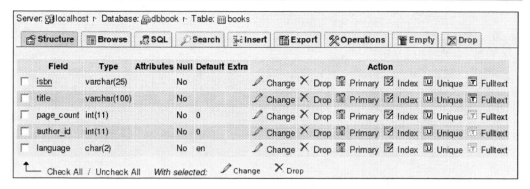

This panel does not allow every possible change to fields. It specifically allows:

- Changing one field structure, using the Change link on a specific field
- Removing a field: Drop
- Adding a field to an existing Primary key
- Setting a non-unique Index or a Unique index on a field
- Setting a Fulltext index (offered only if the field type allows it)

These are quick links that may be useful in specific situations. Keep in mind that they do not replace the full index management panel or the full field structure panel. Both are explained in this chapter.

We can also use the checkboxes to choose fields, and with the appropriate With selected icons, edit the fields or do a multiple field deletion with Drop. The Check All / Uncheck All option permits us to easily check or uncheck all boxes.

TEXT Fields

We will now explore how to use the TEXT field type and the relevant configuration values to adjust for the best possible phpMyAdmin behavior.

First we add a TEXT field called description:

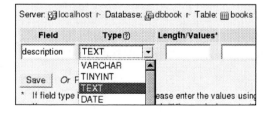

There are three parameters that control the layout of the text area that will be displayed in Insert or Edit mode for the TEXT fields. First, the number of columns and rows for each field is defined by:

```
$cfg['TextareaCols']          = 40;
$cfg['TextareaRows']          = 7;
```

This gives (by default) the following space to work on a TEXT field:

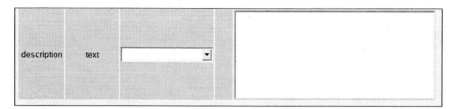

The settings impose only a visual limit on the text area, and a vertical scroll bar is created by the browser, if necessary.

> Although MEDIUMTEXT, TEXT, and LONGTEXT columns can accommodate more than 32K of data, current browsers *cannot* always edit them with the mechanism offered by HTML: a text area. In fact, experimentation has convinced the phpMyAdmin development team to have the product display a warning message if the contents are larger than 32K, telling users that it might not be editable.

For LONGTEXT fields, setting $cfg['LongtextDoubleTextarea'] to TRUE doubles the available editing space.

BLOB (Binary Large Object)

BLOB fields are usually used to hold some binary data (image, sound), even though the MySQL documentation implies that even TEXT fields could be used for the same purpose. However, phpMyAdmin's intention is to work with BLOB fields to hold all binary data.

We will see in Chapter 16, *MIME-Based Transformations* that there are special mechanisms available to go further with BLOB fields, including being able to view some images directly from within phpMyAdmin.

First we add a BLOB field, cover_photo, to our books table:

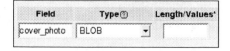

If we now Browse the table, we can see the field length information [BLOB – 0 Bytes] for each BLOB field:

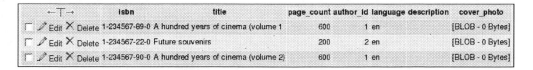

This is because the $cfg['ShowBlob'] configuration directive is set to FALSE by default, thus blocking the display of BLOB contents in Browse and Edit modes (and showing a Binary – do not edit warning). This behavior is intentional—usually we cannot do anything with binary data represented in plain text.

Binary Contents Upload

If we now edit one row, we see the warning *and* a Browse... button. Even though editing is not allowed, we can easily upload a text or binary file into this BLOB column.

Let's choose an image file using the Browse button—for example, the logo_left.png file in the phpMyAdmin/themes/original/img directory—and click Go:

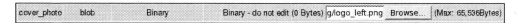

We need to keep in mind some limits for the upload size. First, the BLOB field size is limited to 64K, so phpMyAdmin reminds us of this limit with the Max: 65,536 Bytes warning. Also, there could be limits inherent to PHP itself—see Chapter 8, *Importing Structure and Data*—which would be also taken into account in this maximum size value. We have now uploaded an image inside this field, for a specific row:

If $cfg['ShowBlob'] is set to TRUE, we see the following in the BLOB field:

‰PNG\r\n\Z\n\0\0\0\rIHDR\0\0\0X\0\0\0 -\b*\0\0\0T¦üÒ\0\0\0°rgAMA\0\0±ü ûa‹\0...

> To really *see* the image from within phpMyAdmin, please refer to Chapter 16, *MIME-Based Transformations*.

The $cfg['ProtectBinary'] parameter controls what can be done while editing binary fields (BLOBs and any other field with the binary attribute).

The default value 'blob' permits us to protect against editing of BLOB fields, allowing us to edit other fields marked as binary by MySQL. A value of 'all' would protect against editing even binary fields. A value of FALSE would protect nothing, thus allowing us to edit all fields. If we try the last choice, we see the following in the Edit panel for this row:

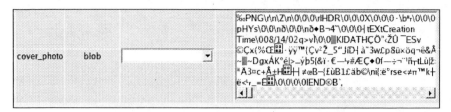

Chances are this is not our favorite image editor! In fact, data corruption may result even if we save this row without touching the BLOB field. But the setting to remove ProtectBinary exists because some users put text in their BLOBs and must be allowed to modify them.

> MySQL BLOB data types are actually similar to their corresponding TEXT data types, with the only difference of being treated as case-sensitive for sorting and comparison purposes. This is why phpMyAdmin can be configured to allow editing of BLOB fields.

ENUM and SET

Both these field types are intended to represent a list of possible values; the difference is that the user can choose only one value from a defined list of values with ENUM, and more than one value with SET. With SET, the multiple values all go into one cell; multiple values do not imply the creation of more than one row of data.

We add a field named genre and define it as an ENUM. For now, we choose to put short codes in the value list, and one of them (F) as the default value:

In the value list, we have to enclose each value within single quotes, unlike in the default value field. In our design, we know that these values stand for *Fantasy*, *Child*, and *Novel*, but for now we want to see the interface's behavior with short codes. In the Insert panel, we now see a radio box interface:

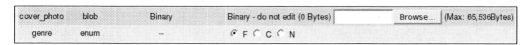

If we decide to have more self-describing codes, we can go back to Structure mode and change the definition for the genre field. In the following example, we do not see the complete value list because the field is not large enough, but what we entered was 'Fantasy','Child','Novel'. We also have to change the default value to one of the possible values, to avoid getting an error message while trying to saving this file structure modification.

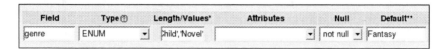

With the modified value list, the Insert panel now looks as follows:

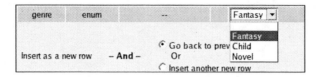

Observe that the previous radio buttons have changed to a select list because of longer possible values.

If we want more than one possible value selected, we have to change the field type to SET. The same value list may be used, but now, using our browser's multiple value selector (usually control-click) we can select more that one value:

For the previous example, we would store only the genre codes in the books table in a normalized data structure, and would rely on another table to store the description for each code. We would not be using a SET or ENUM in this case.

DATE, DATETIME, TIMESTAMP: Calendar Popup

We could use a normal character field to store date or time information, but DATE, DATETIME, and TIMESTAMP are more efficient for this purpose. MySQL checks the contents to ensure valid date and time information. As an added benefit, phpMyAdmin offers a calendar popup for easy data entry.

We will start by adding a DATE field, date_published, to our books table. If we go into Insert mode, we should now see the new field where we could type a date in. A Calendar icon is also available:

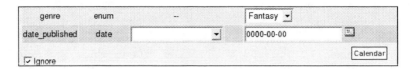

This icon brings a popup, synchronized to this DATE field: if there is already a value in the field, the popup displays accordingly. In our case, the default value 0000-00-00 was in the field, so the calendar shows the current date:

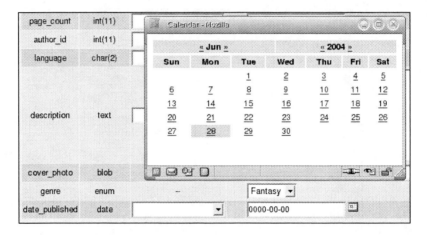

Small symbols on each side of the month and year headers permit easy scrolling through months and years, and a simple click on the date we want transports it to our date_published field.

For a DATETIME or TIMESTAMP field, the popup offers to edit the time part:

Index Management

phpMyAdmin has a number of index management options, which we will cover in this section.

Single-Field Indexes

We have already seen how the Structure panel offers a quick way to create an index on a single field, thanks to some quick links like Primary, Index, and Unique. Under the field list, there is a section of the interface used to manage indexes:

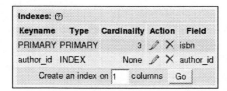

This section has links to edit or delete every index. Here, the Field part lists only one field per index, and we can see that the whole field participates in the index.

We will now add an index on the title. However, we want to restrict the length of this index to reduce the space used by the on-disk index structure. The Create an index on 1 column option is appropriate, so we click Go. In the next screen, we specify the index details as shown in the following screen:

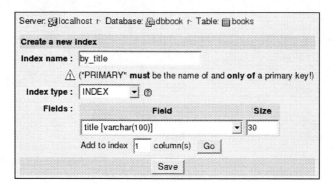

Here is how to fill this panel:

- Index name: A name we invent
- Index type: We can choose INDEX or UNIQUE
- Field: We select the field that is used as the index, which is the title field
- Size: We enter 30 instead of 100 (the complete length of the field) to save space

After saving this panel, we can confirm from the following screenshot that the index is created and does not cover the whole length of the title field:

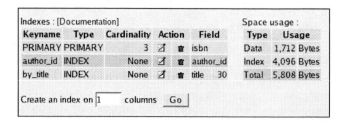

Multi-Field Indexes and Index Editing

In the next example, we will assume that in a future application we will need to find the books written by a specific author in a specific language. It makes sense to expand our author_id index, adding the language field to it.

We click the Edit link (small pencil) on the line containing the author_id index and choose to add one column to this index as shown in the following screenshot:

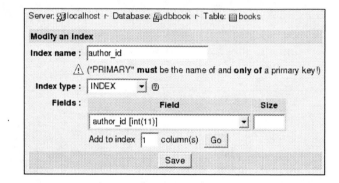

We select the language field on the next panel. This time we do not have to put a size since the whole field will be used in the index:

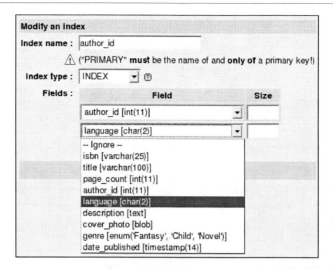

For better documentation, we should also change the key name (author_language would be appropriate). We save this index modification and we are back to:

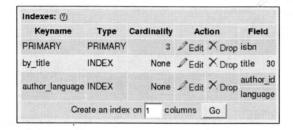

FULLTEXT Indexes

This special type of index allows for full-text searches. It is supported on tables of type MyISAM for VARCHAR and TEXT fields. We can use the Fulltext quick link in the fields list or go to the index management panel and choose Fulltext in the drop-down menu:

We want a FULLTEXT index on the description field so that we are able to locate a book from words present in its description. After the index creation, the index list looks like:

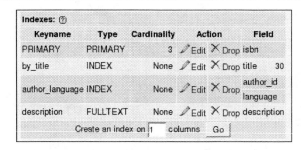

Depending on the MySQL version, we might see 1 as the field length for the newly created index. In fact, MySQL does not support the idea of an index length for FULLTEXT indexes: the index is always on the whole field, but *this* 1 would be the value reported by MySQL.

Table Optimization: EXPLAIN a Query

In this section, we want to get some information about the index that MySQL uses for a specific query, and the performance impact of not having defined an index.

Let's assume we want to use the following query:

```
SELECT  *
FROM  `books`
WHERE author_id = 2 AND language =  'es'
```

We want to know which books written by author 2 are in the es language, our code for Spanish.

To enter this query, we use the SQL link from the database or the table menu, or the SQL query window. We enter this query in the query box and click Go. Whether the query finds any results is not important right now.

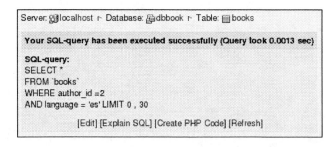

Let's look at the links: [Edit] [Explain SQL] [Create PHP Code] [Refresh]

We will now use the [Explain SQL] link to get information about *which* index (if any) has been used for this query:

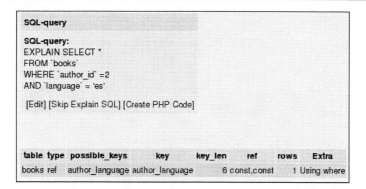

We can see that the EXPLAIN command has been passed to MySQL, telling us that the possible_keys used is author_language. Thus, we know that this index will be used for this type of query. If this index had not existed, the result would have been quite different:

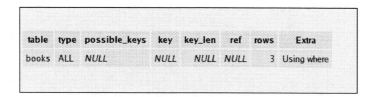

Here, the possible_keys (NULL) and the type (ALL) mean that no index would be used, and that *all* rows would need to be examined to find the desired data. Depending on the total number of rows, this could have a serious impact on the performance. We can ascertain the exact impact by examining the query timing that phpMyAdmin displays on each results page and comparing with or without the index:

Showing rows 0 - 3 (4 total, Query took 0.1977 sec)

However, the difference in time can be minimal if we only have limited test data compared to a real table in production.

Summary

In this chapter we covered:

- How to add fields, including special field types like TEXT, BLOB, ENUM, and SET
- How to use a calendar popup for DATE, DATETIME, and TIMESTAMP fields

- How to upload binary data into a BLOB field
- How to manage indexes (multi-field and full-text)
- How to get feedback from MySQL about which indexes are used in a specific query

Exporting Structure and Data

Keeping good backups is crucial to a project: these constitute up-to-date backups and also intermediary snapshots taken during development and production phases. The export feature of phpMyAdmin can generate backups, and also can be used to send data to other applications.

Dumps, Backups, and Exports

Let's first clarify some vocabulary. In MySQL documentation, you will encounter the term **dump**; in other applications, the term **backup** or **export**. All these terms have the same meaning in the phpMyAdmin context.

MySQL includes **mysqldump**, a command-line utility that can be used to generate export files. But the shell access needed to use command-line utilities is not offered by every host provider. Also, access to the export feature from within the Web interface is more convenient. This is why phpMyAdmin (since version 1.2.0) offers the **Export** feature with more export formats than mysqldump. This chapter will focus on phpMyAdmin's export features.

A full-server export mode exists as well. This mode is only available to a privileged MySQL user, and is discussed in Chapter 18.

Before starting an export, we must have a clear picture of the intended goal of the export, and the following questions may help:

- Do we need the complete database or just some tables?
- Do we need just the structure, just the data, or both?
- Which utility will be used to **import** back the data (not every export format can be imported by phpMyAdmin)?
- Do we want only a subset of the data?
- What is the size of the intended export and the link speed between us and the server?

Database Export

In Database view, click the Export link. The default export panel looks like this:

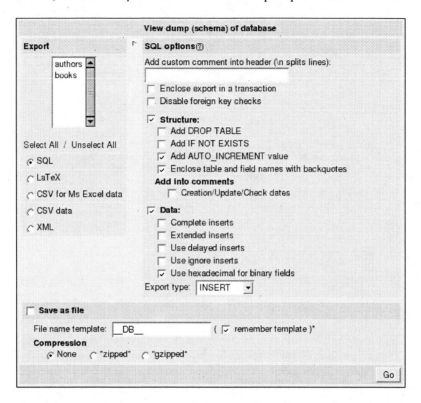

The default values selected here depend on config.inc.php, more specifically on the $cfg['Export'] array of parameters. For example, the $cfg['Export']['format'] parameter is set to 'sql', making the SQL export mode chosen by default.

The export panel comprises three sub-panels. The top panel Export and the bottom panel Save as file are always there, and the third panel varies (using dynamic menu techniques), to show options for the export mode chosen (SQL here).

Export Sub-Panel

This sub-panel contains a table selector, where we choose the table(s) and the format we want. The SQL format is useful for our needs, since it creates standard SQL commands that would work on any SQL server. Other possible formats include **LaTeX**, **Comma-Separated Values (CSV)**, and **XML**. Another format, **Native MS Excel**, is available after further software installation and configuration (see section *Native MS Excel* in this chapter).

Even if we can export from phpMyAdmin into all these formats, only the SQL and CSV formats can be imported back using the current phpMyAdmin version. Use only these two formats for backup.

We shall now discuss the formats (and the options available once they are chosen) that can be selected with the Export sub-panel.

SQL Format

We will start by clicking Select All; we want all the tables. We know that the tables are small, so the on-screen export will not be too large. We then click Go, which produces the following output:

```
-- phpMyAdmin SQL Dump
-- version 2.6.0
-- http://www.phpmyadmin.net
--
-- Host: localhost
-- Generation Time: Jul 05, 2004 at 01:01 PM
-- Server version: 4.0.18
-- PHP Version: 5.0.0-dev
--
-- Database: `dbbook`
--


-- ---------------------------------------------------------


--
-- Table structure for table `authors`
--

CREATE TABLE `authors` (
  `author_id` int(11) NOT NULL default '0',
  `author_name` varchar(30) NOT NULL default '',
  `phone` varchar(30) default NULL,
  PRIMARY KEY  (`author_id`)
) TYPE=MyISAM;

--
-- Dumping data for table `authors`
--

INSERT INTO `authors` VALUES (1, 'John Smith', '111-1111');
INSERT INTO `authors` VALUES (2, 'Maria Sunshine', '222-2222');

-- ---------------------------------------------------------


--
-- Table structure for table `books`
--

CREATE TABLE `books` (
  `isbn` varchar(25) NOT NULL default '',
  `title` varchar(100) NOT NULL default '',
```

```
 `page_count` int(11) NOT NULL default '0',
 `author_id` int(11) NOT NULL default '0',
 `language` char(2) NOT NULL default 'en',
 `description` text NOT NULL,
 `cover_photo` blob NOT NULL,
 `genre` set('Fantasy','Child','Novel') NOT NULL default 'Fantasy',
 `date_published` date NOT NULL default '0000-00-00',
 PRIMARY KEY  (`isbn`),
 KEY `by_title` (`title`(30)),
 FULLTEXT KEY `description` (`description`)
) TYPE=MyISAM;


-- Dumping data for table `books`
--

INSERT INTO `books` VALUES ('1-234567-89-0', 'A hundred years of
cinema (volume 1)', 600, 1, 'en', '', '', '', '0000-00-00');
INSERT INTO `books` VALUES ('1-234567-22-0', 'Future souvenirs', 200,
2, 'en', '', 0x89504e0049454e44ae426082, '', '0000-00-00');
INSERT INTO `books` VALUES ('1-234567-90-0', 'A hundred years of
cinema (volume 2)', 600, 1, 'en', '', '', '', '0000-00-00');
```

In this export example, the data for the second book (starting with 0x8950) has been truncated for brevity. In fact, it would contain the full hexadecimal representation of the cover_photo field of this book.

The first part of the export comprises comments (starting with the -- characters) that detail the utility (and version) that created the file, the date, and other environment information. We then see the CREATE and INSERT queries for each table.

> Starting with version 2.6.0, phpMyAdmin generates ANSI-compatible comments in the export file—the comments start with --. This helps importing the file back on other ANSI SQL-compatible systems. In previous versions, the MySQL-specific '#' character was used.

SQL Options

SQL options are used to define exactly what information the export will contain. We may want to see the structure, the data, or both. Selecting Structure generates the section with CREATE queries, and selecting Data produces INSERT queries:

The options in Structure section are:

- **Add custom comment into header**: We can add our own comments for this export—for example 'Monthly backup'—which will show in the export headers (after the PHP version number). If the comment has more than one line, we must use the special character \n to separate each line.

- **Enclose export in a transaction**: Starting with MySQL 4.0.11, we can use the START TRANSACTION statement. This command, combined with SET AUTOCOMMIT=0 at the beginning and COMMIT at the end, asks MySQL to execute the import—when we will re-import this file back—in one transaction, ensuring all the changes are done as a whole.

- **Disable foreign key checks**: In the export file, we can add DROP TABLE statements. However, normally a table cannot be dropped if it is referenced in a foreign key constraint. This option overrides the verification by adding a SET FOREIGN_KEY_CHECKS=0 to the export file.

- **Add DROP TABLE**: Adds a DROP TABLE IF EXISTS statement before each CREATE TABLE statement, for example DROP TABLE IF EXISTS `authors`;. This way, we can ensure that the export file can be executed on a database in which the same table already exists, updating its structure but destroying previous table contents.

- **Add IF NOT EXISTS**: Adds the IF NOT EXISTS modifier to CREATE TABLE statements, avoiding an error during import if the table already exists.

- **Add AUTO-INCREMENT value**: Puts auto-increment information from the tables into the export, ensuring that the inserted rows in the tables will receive the correct next auto-increment ID value.

- Enclose table and field names with backquotes: Backquotes are the normal way of protecting table and field names that may contain special characters. In most cases it is useful to have them, except if the target server (where the export file will be imported) is running a MySQL version older than 3.23.6, which does not support backquotes.

- Add into comments: Puts (in the form of SQL comments) information that cannot be directly imported, but represents nonetheless valuable human-readable table information. The amount of information here varies depending on the relational system (see Chapter 11) settings. In fact, with an activated relational system, we would get the following choices:

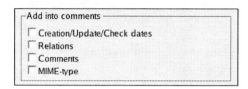

Selecting all these choices would produce this more complete structure export:

```
CREATE TABLE `books` (
  `isbn` varchar(25) NOT NULL default '',
  `title` varchar(100) NOT NULL default '',
  `page_count` int(11) NOT NULL default '0',
  `author_id` int(11) NOT NULL default '0',
  `language` char(2) NOT NULL default 'en',
  `description` text NOT NULL,
  `cover_photo` mediumblob NOT NULL,
  `genre` set('Fantasy','Child','Novel') NOT NULL default 'Fantasy',
  `date_published` date NOT NULL default '0000-00-00',
  PRIMARY KEY (`isbn`),
  KEY `by_title` (`title`),
  KEY `author_id` (`author_id`)
) TYPE=MyISAM COMMENT='Contains book description';


--
-- COMMENTS FOR TABLE `books`:
--   `isbn`
--        `book number`
--   `page_count`
--        `approximate`
--   `author_id`
--        `see authors table`
--


--
-- MIME TYPES FOR TABLE `books`:
--   `cover_photo`
--        `image_jpeg`
--   `date_released`
--        `text_plain`
--   `description`
--        `text_plain`
--
```

```
--
-- RELATIONS FOR TABLE `books`:
--    `author_id`
--       `authors` -> `author_id`
--
```

The options available in the Data section are:

- Complete inserts: Generates the following export for the authors table:

```
INSERT INTO `authors` (`author_id`, `author_name`, `phone`) VALUES
(1, 'John Smith', '+01 445 789-1234');
INSERT INTO `authors` (`author_id`, `author_name`, `phone`) VALUES
(2, 'Maria Sunshine', '+01 455 444-5683');
```

  Notice that every column name is present on every statement. The resulting file is bigger, but will prove more portable on various SQL systems, with the added benefit of being better documented.

- Extended inserts: Packs the whole table data into a single INSERT statement:

```
INSERT INTO `authors` VALUES (1, 'John Smith', '+01 445 789-1234'),
(2, 'Maria Sunshine', '+01 455 444-5683');
```

  This method of inserting data is faster than using multiple INSERTs, but is inconvenient because it makes reading the resultant file harder. Extended inserts also produces a smaller file, but be forewarned that each line of this file is not executable in itself because each line does not have an INSERT statement. If you cannot import the complete file in one operation, you cannot split the file with a text editor and import it chunk by chunk.

- Use delayed inserts: Adds the DELAYED modifier to INSERT statements. This accelerates the INSERT operation because it is queued to the server, which will execute it when the table is not in use. Please note that this is a MySQL non-standard extension, and it's only available for MyISAM and ISAM tables.

- Use ignore inserts: Normally, at import time, we cannot insert duplicate values for keys—this would abort the insert operation. This option adds the IGNORE modifier to INSERT and UPDATE statements, thus skipping the rows which generate duplicate key errors.

- Use hexadecimal for binary fields: A field with the BINARY attribute can have (or not) binary contents. This option makes phpMyAdmin encode the contents of these fields in 0x format. Uncheck this option if the fields are marked BINARY but are nevertheless in plain text, like the mysql.user table.

- Export type: The choices are INSERT, UPDATE, and REPLACE. The most well-known of those types is the default INSERT—using INSERT statements to import back our data. At import time, however, we could be in a situation where a table already exists, has valuable data, and we just want to update the fields that are in the *current* table we are exporting. UPDATE generates statements like UPDATE `authors` SET `author_id` = 1, `author_name` = 'John Smith', `phone` = '111-1111' WHERE `author_id` = '1';—

updating a row when the same primary or unique key is found. The third possibility, REPLACE, produces statements like REPLACE INTO `authors` VALUES (1, 'John Smith', '111-1111'); which act like an INSERT for new rows and updates existing rows, based on primary or unique keys.

Save as file Sub-Panel

In the previous examples, the results of the export operation were displayed on-screen, and of course no compression was made on the data. We can choose to transmit the export file via HTTP by checking the Save as file checkbox. This triggers a Save dialog into the browser, which ultimately saves the file on our local station:

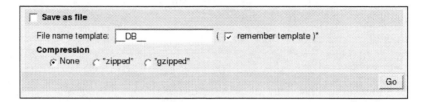

File Name Template

The name of the proposed file will obey the File name template. In this template, we can use the special __DB__ and __TABLE__ placeholders, which will be replaced by the current database or table name (for a single-table export). Note that there are two underscore characters before and after the words. We can also use any special character from the PHP strftime function; this is useful for generating an export file based on the current date or hour. Finally we can put any other string of characters (not part of the strftime special characters), which will be used literally. The file extension is generated according to the type of export. In this case, it will be .sql. Here are some examples for the template:

- __DB__ would generate dbbook.sql
- __DB__-%Y%m%d gives dbbook-20031206.sql

The remember template option, when activated, stores the entered template settings into cookies (for database, table, or server exports) and brings them back the next time we use the same kind of export.

Compression

To save transmission time and get a smaller export file, phpMyAdmin can compress to zip, gzip, or bzip2 formats. phpMyAdmin has native support for the zip format, but gzip and bzip2 formats work only if the PHP server has been compiled with the

--with-zlib or --with-bz2 configuration option, respectively. The following parameters control which compression choices are presented in the panel:

```
$cfg['ZipDump']                  = TRUE;
$cfg['GZipDump']                 = TRUE;
$cfg['BZipDump']                 = FALSE;
```

A system administrator installing phpMyAdmin for a number of users could choose to set all these parameters to FALSE so as to avoid the potential overhead incurred by a lot of users compressing their exports at the same time. This situation usually causes more overhead than if all users were transmitting their uncompressed files at the same time.

In older phpMyAdmin versions, the compression file was built in the web server memory. Some problems caused by this were:

- File generation depended on the memory limits assigned to running PHP scripts.
- During the time the file was generated and compressed, no transmission occurred, so users were inclined to think that the operation was not working and that something had crashed.
- Compression of large databases was impossible to achieve.

The $cfg['CompressOnFly'] parameter (set to TRUE by default) was added to generate (for gzip and bzip2 formats) a compressed file containing more headers. Now, the transmission starts almost immediately. The file is sent in smaller chunks—the whole process consumes much lesser memory.

CSV Data Format

This format is understood by a lot of programs, and you may find it useful for exchanging data. Note that it is a data-only format—no SQL structure here.

The available options are:

- **Fields terminated by**: We put a comma here, which means that a comma will be placed after each field.

- **Fields enclosed by**: We place an enclosing character here (like the quote) to ensure that a field containing the terminating character (comma) is not taken for two fields.

- **Fields escaped by**: If the export generator finds the Fields enclosed by character inside a field, the Fields escaped by character will be placed before it in order to protect it. For example, "John \"The Great\" Smith".

- **Line terminated by**: This decides the character that ends each line. We should use the proper line delimiter here depending on the operating system on which we will manipulate the resulting export file. Here we choose \n for a UNIX-style new line.

- **Replace NULL by**: If the system finds a NULL value in a field, this decides which string to replace it with in the export file.

- **Put fields names at first row**: This gets some information about the meaning of each field. Some programs will use this information to name the column.

Finally we select the authors table.

The result is:

```
"author_id","author_name","phone"
"1","John Smith","+01 445 789-1234"
"2","Maria Sunshine","+01 455 444-5683"
```

CSV for MS Excel Data

This option may have been useful for older versions of Excel, but it is not required any more. Data exported using the CSV option can be imported into recent versions of Excel on both Windows and Macintosh.

LaTeX

LaTeX is a typesetting language. phpMyAdmin can generate a .tex file that represents the table's structure and/or data in sideways tabular format. Note that this file is not directly viewable, and must be further processed or converted for the intended final media.

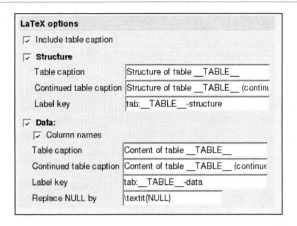

The available options are:

- Include table captions: Display captions to the tabular output

- Structure and Data: The familiar choice to request structure, data, or both

- Table caption: The caption to go on the first page

- Table caption (continued): The caption to go on pages after page one

- Relations, Comments, MIME-type: Other structure information we want to be output. These choices are available if the relational infrastructure is in place (see Chapter 11).

The generated LaTeX file for the data in the authors table looks like this:

```
% phpMyAdmin LaTeX Dump
% version 2.6.0
% http://www.phpmyadmin.net
%
% Host: localhost
% Generation Time: Jul 05, 2004 at 06:13 PM
% Server version: 4.0.18
% PHP Version: 5.0.0-dev
%
% Database: `dbbook`
%

%
% Structure: authors
%
 \begin{longtable}{|l|c|c|c|}
 \caption{Structure of table authors} \label{tab:authors-structure}
\\
 \hline \multicolumn{1}{|c|}{\textbf{Field}} &
\multicolumn{1}{|c|}{\textbf{Type}} &
\multicolumn{1}{|c|}{\textbf{Null}} &
\multicolumn{1}{|c|}{\textbf{Default}} \\ \hline \hline
\endfirsthead
 \caption{Structure of table authors (continued)} \\
```

```
  \hline \multicolumn{1}{|c|}{\textbf{Field}} &
\multicolumn{1}{|c|}{\textbf{Type}} &
\multicolumn{1}{|c|}{\textbf{Null}} &
\multicolumn{1}{|c|}{\textbf{Default}} \\ \hline \hline \endhead
\endfoot \textbf{\textit{author\_id}} & int(11) & No & 0 \\ \hline
author\_name & varchar(30) & No &  \\ \hline
phone & varchar(30) & Yes & NULL \\ \hline
  \end{longtable}

%
% Data: authors
%
  \begin{longtable}{|l|l|l|}
  \hline \endhead \hline \endfoot \hline
  \caption{Content of table authors} \label{tab:authors-data} \\\hline
\multicolumn{1}{|c|}{\textbf{author\_id}} &
\multicolumn{1}{|c|}{\textbf{author\_name}} &
\multicolumn{1}{|c|}{\textbf{phone}} \\ \hline \hline  \endfirsthead
\caption{Content of table authors (continued)} \\ \hline
\multicolumn{1}{|c|}{\textbf{author\_id}} &
\multicolumn{1}{|c|}{\textbf{author\_name}} &
\multicolumn{1}{|c|}{\textbf{phone}} \\ \hline \hline \endhead
\endfoot
1 & John Smith & 111-1111 \\ \hline
2 & Maria Sunshine & 222-2222 \\ \hline
  \end{longtable}
```

XML

This format is very popular nowadays for data exchange. Choosing XML in the Export interface yields no choice for options. What follows is the output for the authors table:

```xml
<?xml version="1.0" encoding="iso-8859-1" ?>
<!--
-
- phpMyAdmin XML Dump
- version 2.5.5-rc2
- http://www.phpmyadmin.net
-
- Host: localhost
- Generation Time: Jan 22, 2004 at 03:21 PM
- Server version: 4.0.11
- PHP Version: 4.3.1
-->
<!--
- Database : `dbbook`
-->
<dbbook>
   <!-- Table authors -->
     <authors>
        <author_id>1</author_id>
        <author_name>John Smith</author_name>
        <phone>111-2222</phone>
        <country_code></country_code>
     </authors>
     <authors>
        <author_id>2</author_id>
        <author_name>Maria Sunshine</author_name>
```

```
        <phone>111-2222</phone>
        <country_code></country_code>
    </authors>
    <authors>
        <author_id>101</author_id>
        <author_name>Melanie Smith</author_name>
        <phone>111-2222</phone>
        <country_code></country_code>
    </authors>
    <authors>
        <author_id>100</author_id>
        <author_name>Paul Smith</author_name>
        <phone>111-2222</phone>
        <country_code></country_code>
    </authors>
</dbbook>
```

Native MS Excel

Starting with version 2.6.0, phpMyAdmin offers an *experimental* module to export directly in .xls format, the native spreadsheet format understood by **MS Excel** and **OpenOffice Calc**. When this support is activated (more on this in a moment), we see a new export choice:

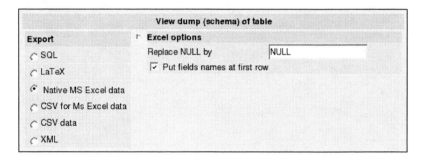

We can optionally put our field names in the first row of the spreadsheet, with Put fields names at first row.

This functionality relies on the PEAR module Spreadsheet_Excel_Writer, which is currently at version 0.8 and generates Excel 5.0 format files. This module is documented at http://pear.php.net/package/Spreadsheet_Excel_Writer, but the complete installation in phpMyAdmin's context is documented here:

1. Ensure that the PHP server has PEAR support (the pear command will fail if we do not have PEAR support). PEAR itself is documented at http://pear.php.net.

2. If we are running PHP in safe mode, we have to ensure that we are allowed to include the PEAR modules. Assuming the modules are located under

/usr/local/lib/php, we should have the line safe_mode_include_dir = /usr/local/lib/php in php.ini.

3. We then install the module with pear -d preferred_state=beta install -a Spreadsheet_Excel_Writer (because the module is currently in beta state). This command fetches the necessary modules over the Internet and installs them into our PEAR infrastructure.

4. We need a temporary directory—under the main phpMyAdmin directory—for the .xls generation. It can be created on a Linux system with mkdir tmp ; chmod o+rwx tmp.

5. We set the $cfg['TempDir'] parameter in config.inc.php to './tmp'.

We should now be able to see the new **Native MS Excel data** export choice.

Table Export

In the Table view, the Export link brings up the export sub-panel for a specific table. It is similar to the database export panel except that there is no table selector. However, there is an additional section for split exports before the Save as file sub-panel.

Split-File Export

The Dump 3 row(s) starting at record # 0 dialog enables us to split the file into chunks. Depending on the exact row size, we can experiment with various values for the number of rows to find how many rows can be put in a single export file before the memory or execution time limits are hit in the web server. We could then use names like books00.sql and books01.sql for our export files.

Selective Exports

At various places in phpMyAdmin's interface, we can export the results we see, or select *which* rows we want to export.

Exporting Partial Query Results

When the results are displayed from phpMyAdmin, an Export link appears at the bottom of the page:

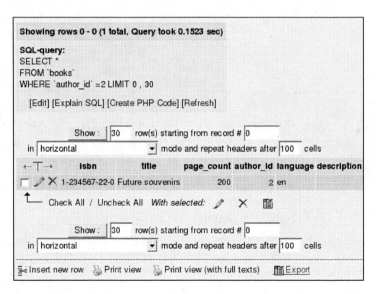

Clicking on this link brings up a special export panel containing the query on the top along with the other table export options:

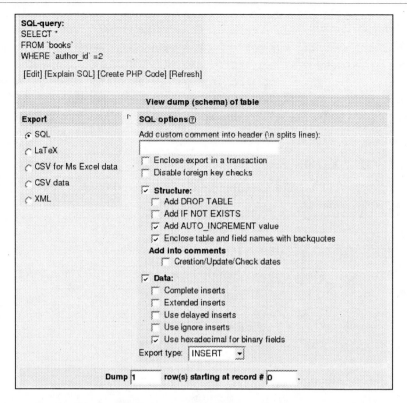

The results of single-table queries can be exported in all the available formats, while the results of multi-table queries can be exported only in CSV, XML, and LaTeX formats.

Exporting and Checkboxes

Anytime we see results (when browsing or searching, for example), we can check the boxes beside the rows we want, and use the With selected: export icon to generate a partial export file with just those rows.

←↑→	isbn	title	page_count	author_id	language	description	cover_photo	genre	date_published
☑ ✎ ✕	1-234567-89-0	A hundred years of cinema (volume 1	600	1	en		[BLOB - 0 Bytes]		0000-00-00
☐ ✎ ✕	1-234567-22-0	Future souvenirs	200	2	en		[BLOB - 4.3 KB]		0000-00-00
☑ ✎ ✕	1-234567-90-0	A hundred years of cinema (volume 2)	600	1	en		[BLOB - 0 Bytes]		0000-00-00

Check All / Uncheck All With selected: ✎ ✕ ▤

Show : 30 row(s) starting from record # 0 Export

Saving the Export File on the Server

Instead of transmitting the export file over the network with HTTP, it is possible to save it directly on the file system of the web server. This could be quicker and less sensitive to execution time limits because the whole transfer from server to client browser is bypassed. Eventually, a file transfer protocol like FTP or SFTP can be used to retrieve the file, since leaving it on the same machine would not provide a good backup protection.

A special directory has to be created on the web server before saving an export file on it. Usually this is a subdirectory of the main phpMyAdmin directory. We will use save_dir as an example. This directory must have special permissions. First, the web server must have write permissions for this directory. Also, if the web server's PHP component is running in safe mode, the owner of the phpMyAdmin scripts must be the same as the owner of save_dir.

On a Linux system, assuming that the web server is running as user apache and the scripts are owned by user marc, the following commands would do the trick:

```
# mkdir save_dir
# chown marc.apache save_dir
# chmod g=rwx save_dir
```

We also have to define the './save_dir' directory name in $cfg['SaveDir']. We are using a path relative to the phpMyAdmin directory here, but an absolute path would work just as well.

The Save as file section will appear with a new Save on server section:

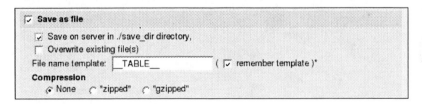

After clicking Go, we will get a confirmation message or an error message (if the web server does not have the required permissions to save the file).

> For saving a file again using the same file name, check the Overwrite existing file(s) box.

Summary

In this chapter:

- We examined the various ways to trigger an export: from the Database view, Table view, or from a results page
- We listed the various available export formats, their options, the possibility of compressing the export file, and the various places where it might be sent

Importing Structure and Data

In this chapter we will learn how to bring back exported data that we might have created for backup or transfer purposes. Exported data may also come from authors of other applications, and could contain the whole foundation structure of these applications and some sample data.

The current phpMyAdmin version can directly import files containing MySQL statements (usually having a `.sql` suffix, but not necessarily so). There is also an interface to the MySQL LOAD DATA INFILE statement, enabling us to load text files containing data, usually called CSV (comma-separated values), although the separator can be another character. The binary field upload covered in Chapter 6 can be classified in the import family.

> Importing and uploading are synonyms in our context.

In phpMyAdmin version 2.5.5, there is no Import menu in the Database view or the Table view that would contain all possible import links, but there is an Import files menu available inside the Query window.

Limits for the Transfer

When we import, the source file is usually on our client machine, so it must travel to the server via HTTP. This transfer takes time and uses resources that might be limited in the web server's PHP configuration.

Instead of using HTTP, we can upload our file to the server using a protocol like FTP, as the *Web-Server Upload Directory* section describes. This method circumvents the PHP server's upload limits.

Time Limits

First, let's consider the time limit. In `config.inc.php`, the `$cfg['ExecTimeLimit']` configuration directive assigns, by default, a maximum execution time of 300 seconds (five minutes) for *any* phpMyAdmin script, including the scripts that process data after the file has been uploaded. A value of 0 removes the limit and in theory gives us infinite time to complete the import operation. If the PHP server is running in safe mode, modifying `$cfg['ExecTimeLimit']` will have no effect, because the limits set in `php.ini` or in user-related web server configuration (like `.htaccess` or virtual host configuration) take precedence over this parameter.

Of course, the time it effectively takes depends on two key factors:

- Web server load
- MySQL server load

> The time taken by the file as it travels between the client and the server does not count as execution time, because the PHP script only starts to execute after the file has been received on the server. So, the `$cfg['ExecTimeLimit']` parameter has an impact only on the time used to process data (like decompression or sending to MySQL server).

Other Limits

Using the `php.ini` file or the web server's virtual host configuration file, the system administrator can control uploads on the server.

The `upload_max_filesize` parameter specifies the upper limit or the maximum file size that can be uploaded via HTTP. This one is obvious, but another less obvious parameter is `post_max_size`. Since HTTP uploading is done via the POST method, this parameter may limit our transfers.

The `memory_limit` parameter is provided to avoid web server child processes from grabbing too much of the server memory—phpMyAdmin also runs as a child process. Thus, the handling of normal file uploads, especially compressed dumps, can be compromised by placing a small value for this parameter. Here, no *preferred* value can be recommended—it depends on the size of uploaded data.

Finally, file uploads must be allowed by setting `file_uploads` to `on`. Otherwise, phpMyAdmin won't even show the Location of the textfile dialog. It would be useless to display this dialog, since the connection would be refused later by the PHP server.

Importing SQL Files

Any file containing MySQL statements can be imported via this mechanism. The dialog is available in the Database view or the Table view, via the SQL sub-page, or in the Query window. The important part to look for is the Location of the textfile dialog:

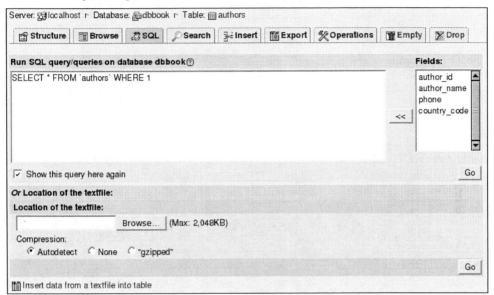

> There is no relation between the currently selected table (here authors) and the actual contents of the SQL file that will be imported. All the contents of the SQL file will be imported, and it is these contents that determine which table or databases are affected. However if the imported file does not contain any SQL statements to select a database, all statements of the imported file will be executed on the currently selected database.

Let's try an import exercise. First we make sure that we have a current SQL export of the books table (as explained in Chapter 7). This export file must contain the structure and data. Then we Drop the books table (yes, really!). We could also simply rename it (see Chapter 10 for the procedure).

Now it is time to import the file back. We should be on a page where we can see the Location of the text file dialog. We just have to hit the Browse button and choose our file.

We can also specify which compression method has been applied to the file or let phpMyAdmin try to auto-detect it. In this case, we use the default Autodetect choice.

To start the import, we click Go:

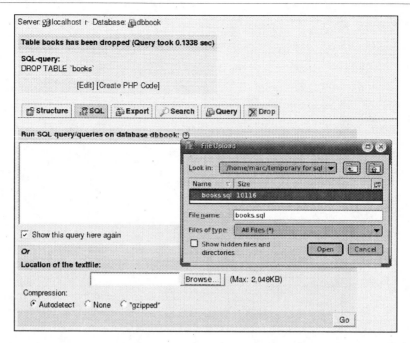

We can confirm the results by verifying the CREATE TABLE statement and the number of affected rows for each INSERT statement. We should also browse our newly created table to confirm the success of the import operation.

The file could be imported in a different database or even MySQL server for testing.

Importing CSV Files

In this section, we will examine how to import CSV files.

Differences Between SQL and CSV Formats

There are some differences between these two formats. The CSV file format contains data *only*, so we must already have an existing table in place. This table does not need to have the same structure as the original table (from which the data comes); the Column names dialog enables us to choose which columns are affected in the target table.

Another difference is that phpMyAdmin relies on the server's LOAD DATA INFILE or LOAD DATA LOCAL INFILE mechanisms to do the actual import, instead of processing the data internally. These statements are the fastest way for importing text in MySQL. They cause MySQL to start a read operation from a file located on the MySQL server (LOAD DATA INFILE) or from another place (LOAD DATA LOCAL INFILE), which, in this context, is always the web server's file system. If the MySQL server is located on a computer other than the web server, we won't be able to use the LOAD DATA INFILE mechanism.

Requirements

Relying on the MySQL server has some consequences. Using LOAD DATA INFILE requires that the logged-in user possess a global FILE privilege. Also, the file itself must be readable by the MySQL server's process.

> Chapter 18 explains phpMyAdmin's interface to privileges management for system administrators.

Using the LOCAL modifier in LOAD DATA LOCAL INFILE must be allowed by the MySQL server and MySQL's client library used by PHP.

Both the LOAD methods are available from the phpMyAdmin LOAD interface, which tries to choose the best possible default option.

Using the LOAD Interface

We will start by generating an authors.csv export file, this time from the authors table. In the CSV export options, we use the default values. We can then Empty the authors table (we still need the table structure).

To find the import dialog sub-page, we have to be in the Table view for the authors table.

The Insert data from a textfile into table exists on a number of pages:

- The Structure page
- The SQL page
- The Import files tab in the Query window

We choose to start it from the SQL page, and the Insert data from a textfile into table link brings up the following dialog:

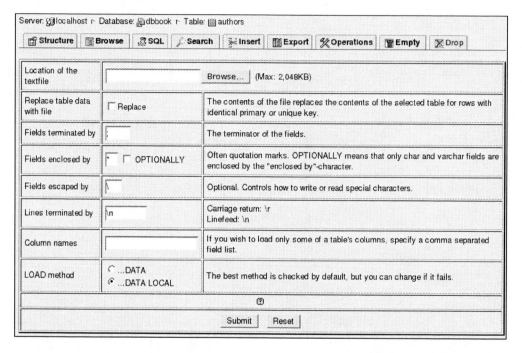

There are many options because the data might come from a number of places; the way fields are encoded and even the end-of-line character might vary depending on the program used to generate the file or the source operating system.

First we see the familiar Location of the textfile question. We choose our authors.csv file and just hit Submit for now; we will explore other options later.

If all goes well, we see the confirmation screen:

This screen shows the exact LOAD DATA LOCAL INFILE statement used. Note that the file used was /tmp/phpU0HGGG and not authors.csv, because our authors.csv file is received by PHP, saved as a temporary file, and then read and loaded by MySQL.

LOAD Options

By default, the LOAD operation will not modify existing data (based on primary or unique keys), but the Replace option instructs phpMyAdmin to add a REPLACE keyword to the generated command, which will modify data if the keys are the same.

We can then specify the character that terminates each field, the character that encloses data, and the character that escapes the enclosing character. Usually this is \. For example, for a double quote enclosing character, if the data field contains a double quote, it must be expressed as "some data \" some other data".

For Lines terminated by, the usual choice is \n for UNIX-based systems, \r\n for DOS or Windows systems, and \r for Mac-based system. If in doubt, we can use a hexadecimal file editor on our client computer (not part of phpMyAdmin) to examine the exact codes.

By default, phpMyAdmin expects a CSV file with the same number of fields and the same field order as the target table, but this can be changed by entering a comma-separated list of column names in Column names, respecting the source file format. For example, let's say our source file only contains the author ID and author name information:

```
"1","John Smith"
"2","Maria Sunshine"
```

We'd have to put author_id, author_name in Column names to match the source file.

Finally, we can choose LOAD format, as discussed earlier.

If the file is too big, there are ways in which we can resolve the situation. If we still have access to the original data, we could use phpMyAdmin to generate smaller CSV export files, choosing the Dump n rows starting at record # n dialog. If this is not possible, we will have to use a text editor to split the file into smaller sections. Another possibility is to use the UploadDir mechanism.

Web-Server Upload Directory

To get around cases where uploads are completely disabled by a web server's PHP configuration or where upload limits are too small, phpMyAdmin can read upload files from a special directory located on the web server's file system. This mechanism is applicable for SQL and CSV imports.

We first specify the directory name of our choice in the $cfg['UploadDir'] parameter; for example, './upload'.

Now, let's go back to the SQL sub-page and see what happens:

This error message is expected since the directory does not exist. It is supposed to be created inside the current phpMyAdmin installation directory. The message might also indicate that the directory exists, but can't be read by the web server (in PHP safe mode, the owner of the directory *and* the owner of the phpMyAdmin-installed scripts must be the same).

Using an SFTP or FTP client, we create the necessary directory and can upload a file there (bypassing any PHP timeouts or upload maximum limits), for example books.sql. Please note that the file itself must bear permissions that allow the web server to read it. In most cases, the easiest way is to allow everyone to read the file.

Refreshing the SQL sub-page brings up the following:

Clicking Go should execute the file.

Importing Compressed Dumps

phpMyAdmin is able to decompress uploaded files. We can choose the compressed mode directly when we choose the file or simply try the Autodetect mode which should normally work. The formats that the program can decompress vary depending on the phpMyAdmin version and *which* extensions are available in the PHP component of the web server.

This feature is also available for the files located in the upload directory. The file names should have extensions like .bz2, .gz, .sql.bz2, or .sql.gz.

> Using the double extensions (.sql.bz2) is a better way to indicate that a .sql file was produced, and then compressed; we see all the steps used to generate this file.

Summary

In this chapter, we learned:

- The various options of phpMyAdmin that allow us to import data
- The different mechanisms involved in importing SQL and CSV files
- The limits that we might hit when trying a transfer
- Some ways of bypassing the limits

Searching Data

Here we present mechanisms that can be used to find the data we are looking for instead of just browsing tables page-by-page and sorting them. This chapter covers single-table and whole database searches. Chapter 13 is a complement to this chapter and presents multi-table query by example.

Single-Table Search

This section describes the Search sub-page where single-table search is available.

Daily Usage of phpMyAdmin

The main usage of the tool for some users is the Search mode for finding and updating data. For this, the phpMyAdmin team has made it possible to define which sub-page is the starting page in Table view, with the $cfg['DefaultTabTable'] parameter. Setting it to 'tbl_select.php' defines the default sub-page to Search.

With this mode, application developers can look for data in ways not expected by the interface they are building, adjusting and sometimes repairing data.

Entering the Search Sub-Page

The Search sub-page can be accessed by clicking the Search link in the Table view. This has been done here for the books table:

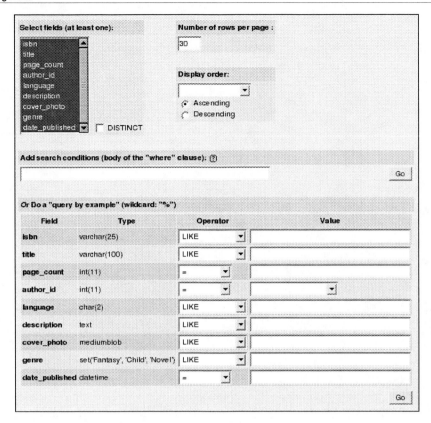

Selection of Display Fields

The first panel facilitates selection of the fields to be displayed in the results:

All fields are selected by default, but we can control-click other fields to make the necessary selections.

Here are the fields of interest to us in this example:

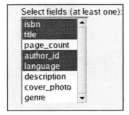

We can also specify the number of rows per page in the textbox just below the field selection. The Add search conditions box will be explained in the *Applying a WHERE Clause* section later in this chapter.

Search Criteria by Field: Query by Example

The main usage of the Search panel is to enter criteria for some fields so as to retrieve only the data in which we are interested. This is called Query by example because we give an example of what we are looking for. Our first retrieval will concern finding the book with ISBN 1-234567-89-0. We simply enter this value in the isbn box and choose the = operator:

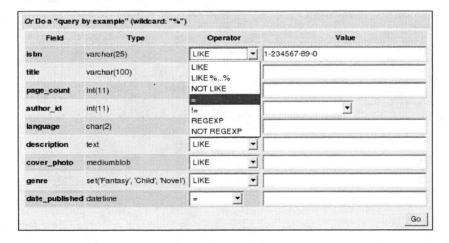

Clicking on Go gives the results shown in the following screenshot. The four fields displayed are those selected in the Select fields dialog:

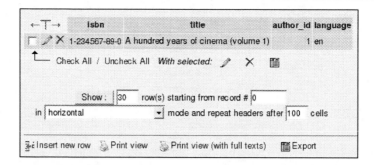

This is a standard results page. If the results ran in pages, we could navigate through them *and* edit and delete data during the process for the *subset we chose*. Another feature of phpMyAdmin is that the fields used as the criteria are highlighted by changing the border color of the columns to better reflect their importance on the results page. It isn't necessary to specify that the isbn column be displayed. We could have selected only the title column for *display* and selected the isbn column as a *criterion*.

Print View

We see the Print view and Print view (with full texts) links on the results page. These links produce a more formal report of the results (without the navigation interface) directly to the printer. In our case, using Print view would produce the following:

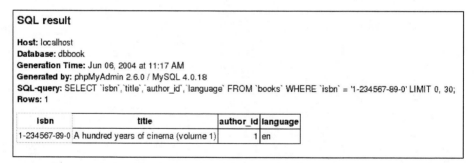

This report contains information about the server, database, time of generation, version of phpMyAdmin, version of MySQL, and the SQL query used. The other link, Print view (with full texts) would print the contents of TEXT fields in its entirety.

Wildcard Searching

Let's assume we are looking for something less precise: all books with 'cinema' in their title. First, we go back to the search page. For this type of search, we will use SQL's LIKE operator. This operator accepts wildcard characters: the % character (which matches any number of characters) and the underscore (_) character (which matches a single character). Thus we can use %cinema% to let phpMyAdmin find any substring that matches the word 'cinema'. If we left out both wildcard characters, we will get exact matches with only that single word.

Since phpMyAdmin 2.6.0, this substring matching has been made easier to access, by adding it to the Operator dropdown. We only have to enter the word cinema and use the operator LIKE %...% to perform that match. We should avoid using this form of the LIKE operator on big tables (thousands of rows), since MySQL does not use an index for data retrieval in this case, leading to wait time that could add up to half an hour (or more). This is why this operator is not the default one in the drop-down list, even though this method of searching is commonly used on smaller tables.

In versions prior to phpMyAdmin 2.6.0, we need to manually insert the % characters to obtain '%cinema%', and use the LIKE operator from the drop-down list.

We also specify that the results be sorted (in an ascending order) by title. Here is a screenshot showing how we ask a search on cinema with the operator LIKE %...%:

Or Do a "query by example" (wildcard: "%")

Field	Type	Operator	Value
isbn	varchar(25)	LIKE	
title	varchar(100)	LIKE %...%	cinema
page_count	int(11)	=	
author_id	int(11)	=	
language	char(2)	LIKE	
description	text	LIKE	
cover_photo	mediumblob	LIKE	
genre	set('Fantasy', 'Child', 'Novel')	LIKE	
date_published	datetime	=	

Go

> The LIKE operator can be used for other types of wildcard searching, for example History%—which would search for this word at the beginning of title. This form of the LIKE query also has the benefit of using an index, if MySQL finds one that speeds up data retrieval.

Using either of these methods of doing the query gives the following results:

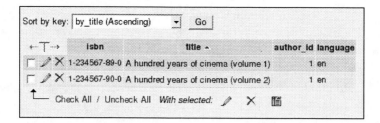

Wildcard characters available are the % character (which matches any number of characters) and the underscore (_) character (which matches a single character).

Combining Criteria

We can use multiple criteria for the same query (for example, to find all English books of more than 300 pages). We see here that there are more comparison choices because of the page_count field being numeric:

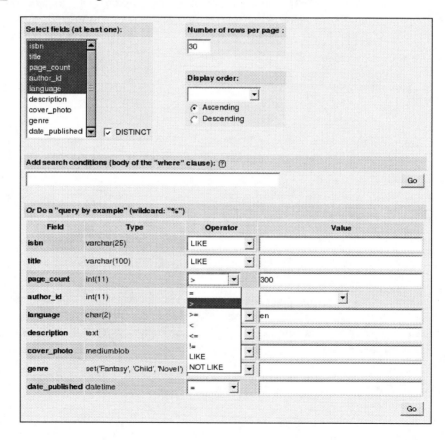

Applying a WHERE Clause

Sometimes we may want to enter a search condition that is *not* offered in the Function list of the Query by example section; the list cannot contain every possible variation available in the language. Let's say we want to find all English or French books. For this, we can use the Add search conditions section:

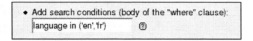

> The complete search expression is generated by combining the search conditions, a logical AND, and the other criteria entered in the Query by example lines.

We could have a more complex list of search conditions that would be entered in the same textbox, possibly with brackets and operators like AND or OR.

A Documentation link points to the MySQL manual, where we can see a huge choice of available functions (each function is applicable for a specific field type).

Obtaining DISTINCT Results

Sometimes we want to avoid getting the same results more than once. For example, to know in which cities we have clients, displaying each city name *once* is enough. Here we want to know the page counts of our books. In the Select Fields dialog, we choose just the page_count field and we check DISTINCT:

Clicking on Go produces the following:

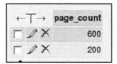

> Using DISTINCT we only see the two page counts '200' and '600' once. Without this option, the row containing '200' would have appeared twice.

Complete Database Search

In the previous examples, searching was limited to one table. This assumes knowledge of the exact table (and columns) where the necessary information might be stored.

When the data is hidden somewhere in the database or when the *same* data can be in various columns (for example, a title column or a description column), it is easier to use the database-search method.

We enter the Search page in the Database view for the dbbook database:

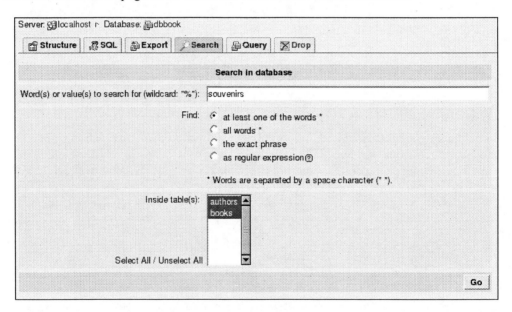

In the Word(s) or value(s) section, we enter what we want to find. The % wildcard character can prove useful here. We enter souvenirs.

In the Find section, we specify how to treat the values entered: we might need to find any of the words entered, all the words (in no particular order), or the exact phrase (words in the same order, somewhere in a column). Another choice is to use a regular expression, which is a more complex way of doing pattern matching. We will keep the default value at least one of the words.

We can choose the tables to restrict the search, or select all tables. As we only have two (small) tables, we select them both.

As the search will be done on each row of every table selected, we might hit some time limits if the number of rows or tables is too big.

Clicking Go finds the following for us:

Search results for "*souvenirs*" (at least one of the words):

- 0 match(es) inside table *authors*
- 1 match(es) inside table *books* Browse Delete

Total: *1* match(es)

This is an overview of the number of matches and the relevant tables. We might get some matches in tables in which we are not interested—however, for the matches that look promising, we can Browse the results page, or even Delete the found rows.

Summary

This chapter covered:

- Single-table search, with query by example criteria and additional criteria specification
- Selecting displayed values and ordering results
- Wildcard searching
- Full database searching

10
Table Operations

In the previous chapters, we dealt mostly with table fields. In this chapter, we will learn how to perform some operations that influence tables as a whole. We will cover table attributes and how to modify them, and also discuss multi-table operations.

In the Table view, various links that enable table operations have been put together on one sub-page: Operations. Here is an overview of the page:

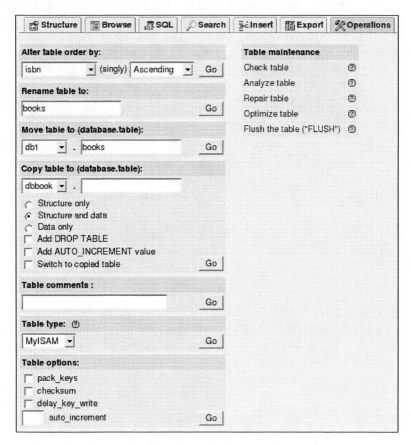

Table Maintenance

During the lifetime of a table, it repeatedly gets modified and so grows and shrinks. Outages may occur on the server, leaving some tables in a damaged state.

Using the Operations sub-page, we can perform various operations, but not every operation is available for every table type:

- Check table: Scans all rows to verify that deleted links are correct. Also, a checksum is calculated to verify the integrity of the keys; we should get an 'OK' message if everything is all right.

- Analyze table: Analyzes and stores the key distribution; this will be used on subsequent JOIN operations to determine the order in which the tables should be joined.

- Repair table: Repairs possibly corrupted data; note that the table might be so corrupted that we cannot even go into Table view for it! In such a case, refer to the *Multi-Table Operations* section for the procedure to repair it.

- Optimize table: This is useful when the table contains overhead. After massive deletions of rows or length changes for VARCHAR fields, lost bytes remain in the table. phpMyAdmin warns us in various places (for example, in the Structure view) if it feels the table should be optimized. This operation is a kind of defragmentation for the table—available if the table type is MyISAM or Berkeley DB.

- Flush table: This must be done when there have been lots of connection errors and the MySQL server blocks further connections. Flushing will clear some internal caches and allow normal operations to resume.

- Defragment table: Random insertions or deletions in an InnoDB table fragment its index. The table should be periodically defragmented for faster data retrieval.

> The operations are based on the underlying MySQL queries available— phpMyAdmin is only calling those queries.

Changing Table Attributes

Attributes are the various properties of a table. This section discusses the settings for various table attributes.

Table Type

The first attribute we can change is the Table type:

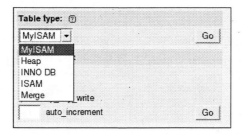

This controls the whole behavior of the table: its location (on-disk or in-memory), the index structure, and whether it supports transactions and foreign keys. The drop-down list may vary depending on the table types supported by our MySQL server.

Changing the table type may be a long operation if the number of rows is large.

Table Comments

This dialog allows us to enter comments for the table. These comments will be shown at appropriate places (for example, under the Table view menu and in the export file).

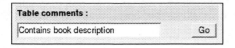

The default value of $cfg['ShowTooltipAliasDB'] and $cfg['ShowTooltipAliasTB'] (FALSE) produces the behavior we have seen earlier: the true database and table names are displayed in the left panel and in the Database view for the Structure sub-page. Comments appear when the mouse pointer is moved over a table name.

If one of these parameters is set to TRUE, the corresponding items (database names for DB and table names for TB) will be shown only as their comments instead of showing their names. This time, the mouse-over shows the true name for the item. This is convenient when the real table names are not meaningful.

There is another possibility for $cfg['ShowTooltipAliasTB']: the 'nested' value. Here is what happens if we use this feature:

- The true table name is displayed in the left panel.
- The table comment (for example project__) is interpreted as the project name and is displayed as such—please refer to the *Nested Display of Tables Within a Database* section in Chapter 3.

Table Order

MySQL applies a default order when we Browse a table without specifying a sort order. This default table order can be changed with the Alter table order by dialog. We can choose any field, and the table will be reordered *once* on this field. We choose author_id in the example, and after clicking Go, the table gets sorted on this field.

This default ordering will last as long as there are no changes in the table (no insertions, deletions, or updates). This is why phpMyAdmin shows the (singly) warning.

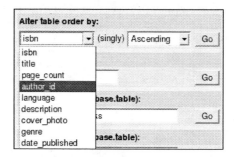

After the sort has been done on author_id, books for author 1 will be displayed first, followed by the books for author 2, and so on (we are talking about a default browsing of the table without explicit sorting). We can also specify the sort order—Ascending or Descending.

If we insert another row, describing a new book from author 1, and then click Browse, the book will not be displayed along with the other books for this author because the sort was done before the insertion.

Table Options

Other attributes that influence the table's behavior may be specified using the Table options dialog:

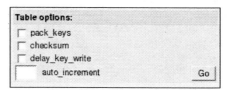

The options are:

- pack_keys: Setting this attribute results in a smaller index; this can be read faster but takes more time to update. Available for MyISAM and ISAM table types.

- checksum: This makes MySQL compute a checksum for each row. This results in slower updates, but easier finding of corrupted tables. Available for MyISAM only.

- delay_key_write: This instructs MySQL to not write the index updates immediately but queue them for later, which improves performance. Available for MyISAM only.

- auto-increment: This changes the auto-increment value.

Rename, Move, and Copy Table

The Rename operation is the easiest to understand: the table simply changes its name and stays in the same database.

The Move operation (shown in the following screen) can manipulate a table in two ways: change its name and *also* the database in which it is stored:

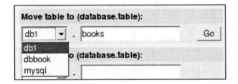

Moving a table is not directly supported by MySQL, so phpMyAdmin has to create the table in the target database, copy the data, and then finally drop the source table.

The Copy operation leaves the original table intact and copies its structure or data (or both) to another table, possibly in another database. Here, the books-copy table will be an exact copy of the books source table. After the copy, we will stay in the Table view for the books table unless we selected Switch to copied table.

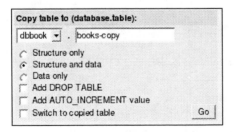

The Structure only copy is done to create a test table with the same structure.

Append Data to Table

The Copy dialog may also be used to append (add) data from a table to another. Both tables must have the same structure. This operation is achieved by entering the table to which we want to copy the data of the current table and choosing Data only.

An example of when we would want to append data is when book data comes from various sources (various publishers), is stored in more than one table, and we want to aggregate all the data to one place.

Multi-Table Operations

In the Database view, there is a checkbox next to each table name and a drop-down menu under the table list. This enables us to quickly choose some tables and perform an operation on all those tables at once. Here we select the books-copy and the books tables, and choose the Check operation for these tables.

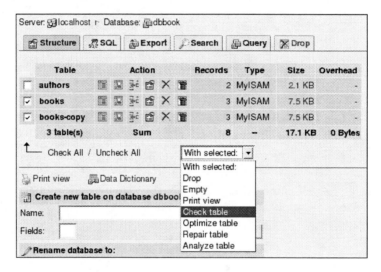

We could also quickly select or deselect all the checkboxes with Check All / Uncheck All.

Repairing an "In Use" Table

The multi-table mode is the only method (unless we know the exact SQL query to type) for repairing a corrupted table. Such tables may be shown with the in use flag in the database list. Users seeking help in the support forums for phpMyAdmin often receive this tip from experienced phpMyAdmin users.

Summary

This chapter covered the operations we can perform on whole tables, and included:

- Table maintenance operations for table repair and optimization
- Changing various table attributes
- Table movements, including renaming and moving to another database
- Multi-table operations

Relational System

Welcome to the part of the book where we start to cover advanced features. The relational system allows users to do more with phpMyAdmin, as we will see in the following chapters. This specific chapter explains how to install the linked-tables infrastructure, which is a prerequisite for the advanced features, and explains how to define inter-table relations.

Relational MySQL?

When application developers use PHP and MySQL to build web interfaces or other data manipulation applications, they usually establish relations between tables, using the underlying SQL queries. For example, 'get an invoice and all its items' and 'get all books by an author'.

In the first versions of phpMyAdmin, MySQL was storing information about *which* table belonged to *which* database, but the relational data structure (how tables relate to each other) was not stored into MySQL. Relations were temporarily made by the applications to generate meaningful results—*the relations were in our heads*.

This was considered a shortcoming of MySQL by phpMyAdmin developers and users, and so the team started to build an infrastructure to support relations. The infrastructure evolved to support a growing array of special features. We can describe this infrastructure as **metadata** (data about data).

phpMyAdmin 2.2.0 already had the **bookmarks** feature (being able to recall frequently used queries, described in Chapter 14), but version 2.3.0 generalized the metadata system. Subsequent versions built on this facility, the latest addition being the 2.5.x family with its MIME-based transformations (described in Chapter 16).

InnoDB

A new MySQL table type (**InnoDB**) became available during phpMyAdmin's development. The InnoDB sub-system has its own webpage at http://www.innodb.com.

Since the InnoDB sub-system must be made active by a system administrator, it may not be available on every MySQL server. Whenever possible, we should use InnoDB table type because:

- It supports referential integrity based on foreign keys, which are the keys in a foreign (or reference) table. By contrast, using only phpMyAdmin's internal relations (discussed later) brings no automatic referential integrity verification.
- InnoDB tables exported definitions contain the defined relations, and are thus easily imported back, for better cross-server interoperability.

InnoDB's foreign key feature can effectively replace—for InnoDB tables only—the part of phpMyAdmin's infrastructure that deals with relations. We will see how phpMyAdmin interfaces to the InnoDB foreign key system.

> The other parts of phpMyAdmin's infrastructure (for example, bookmarks) have no equivalent in InnoDB or MySQL, and thus they are still needed to access the complete phpMyAdmin feature set.

Linked-Tables Infrastructure

The relational system's infrastructure is stored in tables that follow a predetermined structure. The data in these tables is generated and maintained by phpMyAdmin on the basis of our actions from the interface.

Location of the Infrastructure

There are two possible places to store these tables:

- In a user's database because every web developer owning a database should be able to benefit from these features.
- In a dedicated database, which we call the pmadb (phpMyAdmin database). In a multi-user installation (discussed later), this database may be accessible for a number of users while keeping the metadata private.

Because this infrastructure does not exist by default—and because phpMyAdmin's developers want to promote it—the interface displays the following error message for every database when in the Database view:

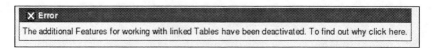

Installing Linked-Tables Infrastructure

The previous error message is displayed even if only a part of the infrastructure is lacking. On a fresh installation, of course, all parts are lacking: our database has not yet heard of phpMyAdmin and needs to be outfitted with this infrastructure. Following the here link of this message brings up the following explanation:

> The message is the same regardless of the current database (here, dbbook) because the infrastructure is shared for all our databases and tables (or all users on a multi-user installation).

As the previous screenshot suggests, the PMA Database is not OK. It's important to realize that the relational system will work only if two conditions are met:

- Proper definitions are present in config.inc.php
- The corresponding tables (and maybe the database) are created

To create the necessary structure matching our current version of phpMyAdmin, a command file called create_tables.sql is available in the scripts subdirectory of the phpMyAdmin installation directory. However, we should not blindly execute it before understanding the possible choices: multi-user installation or single-user installation.

Multi-User Installation

In this setup, we will have a distinct database (pmadb) to store the metadata tables, and our control user will have specific rights to this database. Each user will enter his or her login name and password, which will be used to access his or her databases. However, whenever pmadb has to be accessed, phpMyAdmin will use the control user's privileges.

We first ensure that the control user pma has been created as explained in Chapter 2, and that its definition in config.inc.php is appropriate:

```
$cfg['Servers'][$i]['controluser']    = 'pma';
$cfg['Servers'][$i]['controlpass']    = 'bingo';
```

Then we use the scripts/create_tables.sql file to create the phpmyadmin database, assign proper rights to user pma, and populate the database with all the necessary tables. Before using this script, please have a look in the scripts directory. There might be other scripts available for different MySQL versions—for example, phpMyAdmin 2.6.0 has scripts/create_tables_mysql_4_1_2+.sql, which should be used instead of create_tables.sql for MySQL version 4.1.2 and higher.

> Be warned that this script will erase the phpmyadmin database if it exists, destroying all metadata about relations.

A possible method to execute this script is to use the technique described in Chapter 8 (*Importing Structure and Data*), using the SQL sub-page and the file selector. For this to work, we must have the create_tables.sql script somewhere on our workstation. After the creation, the left panel looks like this:

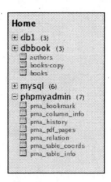

It is now time to adjust all the relational-features related parameters in config.inc.php. Here we use the default values mentioned in the comments inside the file; these database and table names are the ones that were just created:

```
$cfg['Servers'][$i]['pmadb']          = 'phpmyadmin';
$cfg['Servers'][$i]['bookmarktable']  = 'pma_bookmark';
$cfg['Servers'][$i]['relation']       = 'pma_relation';
$cfg['Servers'][$i]['table_info']     = 'pma_table_info';
$cfg['Servers'][$i]['table_coords']   = 'pma_table_coords';
$cfg['Servers'][$i]['pdf_pages']      = 'pma_pdf_pages';
$cfg['Servers'][$i]['column_info']    = 'pma_column_info';
$cfg['Servers'][$i]['history']        = 'pma_history';
```

> As table names are case sensitive, we must use the same names as the tables created by the installation script. We are free to change the table names (see the right-hand part of the configuration directives listed) provided we change them accordingly in the database.

Each table has a specific function:

- pmadb: Defines which database all the tables are located.

- bookmarktable: This is where the bookmarks will be kept (see Chapter 14).

- relation: Defines inter-table relations, as used in many of phpMyAdmin's features.

- table_info: Contains the display field (explained later in this chapter).

- table_coords and pdf_pages: Contain the metadata necessary for drawing a schema of the relations in PDF format (see Chapter 15).
- column_info: Used for column-commenting and MIME-based transformations (see Chapter 16).
- history: Contains SQL query history information (explained in Chapter 12).

Between each phpMyAdmin version, the infrastructure may be enhanced (changes are explained in Documentation.html). This is why phpMyAdmin has various checks to ascertain the structure of tables. If we know that we are using the latest structure, $cfg['Servers'][$i]['verbose_check'] can be set to FALSE to avoid checks, thereby slightly increasing phpMyAdmin's speed.

The installation is now complete; we will test the features in the coming sections and chapters. We can do a quick check by going back to the Home page: the warning message should be gone.

Single-User Installation

Even if we are entitled to only one database by the system administrator, we still can use all the relational features of phpMyAdmin.

In this setup, we will use our normal database (let's assume its name is dbbook) to store the metadata tables and will define our own login name (marc) as the control user in config.inc.php:

```
$cfg['Servers'][$i]['controluser']   = 'marc';
$cfg['Servers'][$i]['controlpass']   = 'bingo';
```

The next step is to modify the local copy of the scripts/create_tables.sql file to populate our database with all the needed tables. They will have the prefix pma_ to make them easily recognizable. Please also read in the *Multi-User Installation* section the remark about other scripts possibly available in the scripts directory.

Be warned that this script will erase the special tables if they exist, destroying all metadata about relations.

The first modification is to remove the comment lines (starting with two dash (-) characters) to make sure they do not interfere (in some phpMyAdmin versions, the import routine does not understand them). Then we remove the following lines:

```
DROP DATABASE `phpmyadmin`;
CREATE DATABASE `phpmyadmin`;

USE phpmyadmin;

GRANT SELECT, INSERT, DELETE, UPDATE ON `phpmyadmin`.* TO
    'pma'@localhost;
```

This is done because we won't be using the phpmyadmin database or the pma control user.

We are now ready to execute the script. There are two ways of doing this:

- Since we already have the script in our editor, we can just copy the lines and paste them in the query box of the SQL sub-page.

- Another way is to use the technique shown in Chapter 8 (*Importing Structure and Data*), with the SQL sub-page and the file selector. We select the create_tables.sql script that we just modified.

After the creation, the left panel shows us the special pma_ tables along with our normal tables:

The last step is to adjust in config.inc.php all the parameters that relate to the relational features. Except for the database name in the pmadb parameter, we use the default values mentioned in the comments inside the file:

```
$cfg['Servers'][$i]['pmadb']          = 'dbbook';
```

Relation View

After the installation of the linked-tables infrastructure, there are now more options available in the Database view and the Table view. We will now examine a new link in the Table view: Relation view. This view is used to:

- Define the relations of the current table to other tables
- Choose the display field
- Define column-specific comments

Since our goal here is to create a relation between the books table (which contains the author ID) and the authors table (which describes each author by an ID), we start on the Table view for the books table and click the Relation view link.

Internal phpMyAdmin Relations

Since the books table is in MyISAM format, we see the following screen (otherwise, the display would be different, as explained in the *InnoDB Relations* section later):

This screen allows us to create Internal relations (stored in the pma_relation table), because MySQL itself does not have any relational notion for MyISAM tables. The double-dash (--) characters indicate that there are *no* relations (links) to any foreign table.

Defining the Relation

We can relate each field of the books table to a field in another table (or in the same table, because self-referencing relations are sometimes necessary). The interface finds the unique and non-unique keys in all tables of the same database and presents the keys in dropdowns. The appropriate choice here is to select for the author_id field the corresponding author_id field from the authors table. This is also called *defining the foreign key*.

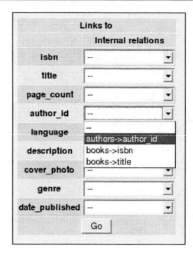

We then click Go, and the definition is saved in phpMyAdmin's infrastructure. To remove the relation, we just come back to the screen, select the double-dash choice, and hit Go.

Defining the Display Field

The primary key of our authors table is the author_id, which is a unique number that we made up just for key purposes. Another field in our table represents the authors: the name. It would be interesting to see the author's name as an informative description of each row of the books table. This is the purpose of the **display field**. We should normally define a display field for each table that participates in a relation as a foreign table.

We will see how this information is displayed in the *Benefits of the Defined Relations* section. We now go in Relation view for the authors table (which is the foreign table in this case) and specify the display field. We choose author_name as the display field:

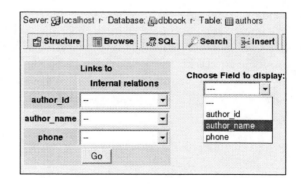

phpMyAdmin offers to define only one display field for a table, and this field is used in all the relations where this table is used as a foreign table.

The definition of this relation is now done. Please note that although we did not relate any of the fields in the authors table to another table, it can be done. For example, we could have a country code in this table and could create a relation to the country code of a country table.

We will discuss the benefits of having defined this relation in a later section, but first, we will see what happens if our tables are of InnoDB type.

InnoDB Relations

The InnoDB table type offers us a foreign key system. To try it, we will first switch our books *and* authors tables to InnoDB type. We can do this in the Table view from the Operations sub-page. We start by doing this for the authors table:

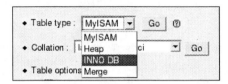

A problem might arise when changing the table type of books table to InnoDB—we have a FULLTEXT index in this table, and some versions of MySQL do not support it for the InnoDB table type. We have to remove the FULLTEXT index if we receive the following error message:

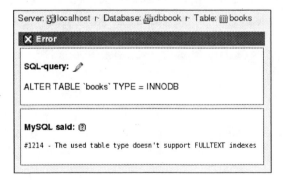

Let's assume that we have done that and subsequently switched the books table to InnoDB.

The foreign key system in InnoDB maintains integrity between the related tables, and so we cannot add a non-existent author ID in the books table. In addition, actions are programmable when DELETE or UPDATE operations are performed on the master table (in our case, books).

Opening the books table and entering the Relation view now displays a different page:

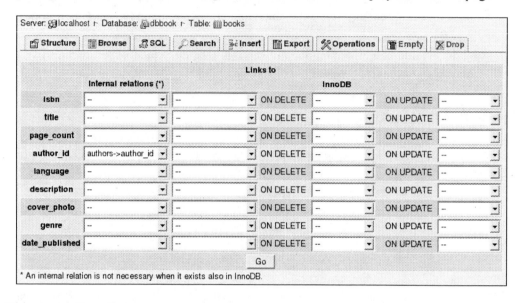

This page tells us that:

- We have an internal relation defined for author_id to authors table.
- We don't yet have any InnoDB relations defined.
- We will be able to remove the internal relation, when the same relation has been defined in InnoDB. In fact, phpMyAdmin advises us that the internal relation is not necessary when it also exists in InnoDB, and so, it would be better to remove it.
- ON DELETE and ON UPDATE options are available for InnoDB relations.

The page might also tell us that our MySQL version is not up to date (it needs to be 4.0.13 or later). One of the implications of this: we would not be able to remove a relation defined in InnoDB. This is why phpMyAdmin could be giving us this friendly (and crucial!) advice.

In the possible choices for related key, we see the keys defined in other InnoDB tables.

Let's try to remove the internal relation for the author_id field and add (even though it won't work) an InnoDB-type relation for the author_id field:

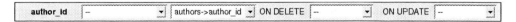

author_id [-- ▼] [authors->author_id ▼] ON DELETE [-- ▼] ON UPDATE [-- ▼]

Clicking Go generates an error message: No index defined! (author_id). This is because foreign key definitions in InnoDB can be done only if *both* fields are defined as indexes (there are also other constraints explained in the MySQL manual).

Thus, we come back to the Structure page for the books table and add an ordinary index (non-unique) to author_id:

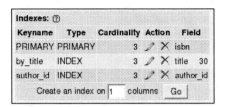

In Relation view, we can again try to add the relation we wanted—it works this time!

We can also set some actions with ON DELETE and ON UPDATE options. For example, ON DELETE CASCADE would make MySQL automatically delete all rows in the related (foreign) table when the corresponding row is deleted from the parent table. This would be useful, for example, when the parent table is 'invoices' and the foreign table is 'invoice-items'.

> If we have not done so already, we should define the 'display field' for the authors table, as explained in the *Internal phpMyAdmin Relations* section.

In the current phpMyAdmin version (2.6.0), we cannot see tables from a different database in order to define a relation to them.

InnoDB Tables Without Linked-Tables Infrastructure

Starting with phpMyAdmin 2.6.0, we see the Relation View link on the Structure page of a InnoDB table even though the linked-tables infrastructure is not installed. This brings us to a screen where we can define the foreign keys—here for the books table.

Please note that if we choose this way, the 'display field' for the linked table (here authors) cannot be defined—it belongs to the phpMyAdmin's infrastructure—so we would lose one of the benefits (seeing the foreign key's associated description).

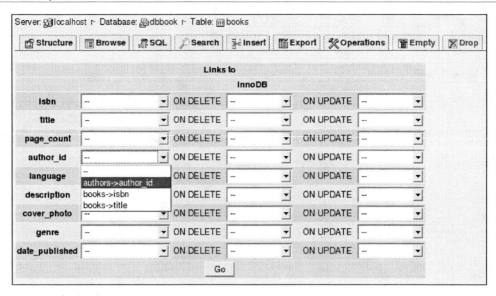

Benefits of the Defined Relations

In this section we will look at the benefits that we can currently test; other benefits will show up in Chapter 13 (*Multi-Table Query Generator*) and Chapter 15 (*System Documentation*). Some other benefits of the linked-tables infrastructure will appear in Chapter 14 (*Bookmarks*) and Chapter 16 (*MIME-Based Transformations*).

These benefits are available for both internal and InnoDB relations.

Foreign Key Information

Let's Browse the books table. We see that the related key (author_id) is now a link.

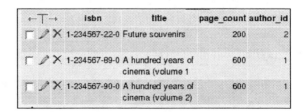

Moving the mouse pointer over any author_id value reveals the author's name (as defined by the display field of the authors table):

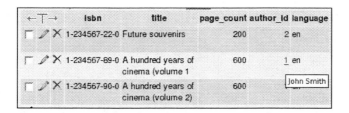

Clicking on the author_id brings us to the relevant table, authors, for this specific author:

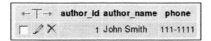

Drop-Down List of Foreign Keys

In Insert mode (or in Edit mode), we now see a drop-down list of the possible keys for each field that has a relation defined. The list contains the keys and the description (display field) in both orders: key to display field *and* display field to key. This enables us to use the keyboard and type the first letter of either the key or the display field:

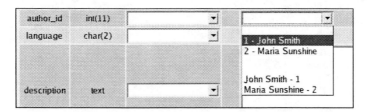

Only the key (in this case 1) will be stored in the books table. The display field is only there to assist us.

This drop-down list will appear if there are a maximum of 200 rows in the foreign table. For foreign tables bigger than that, a distinct window appears: the browseable foreign-table window.

Browseable Foreign-Table Window

We cannot use our current books and authors tables to illustrate this mechanism—they have very few entries. We will use a table called orders with a column software_id related to the ID column of the table software. In Insert mode for the orders table, we see a small table-shaped icon for software_id, as shown in the screenshot that follows:

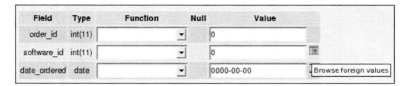

This icon opens another window presenting the values of the table software, and a page selector. On the left, the values are sorted by key value (here, the id column) and on the right, they are sorted by description:

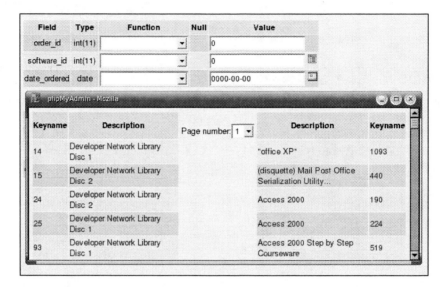

Choosing one of the values—by clicking either a key value or a description—closes this window and brings the value back to the software_id column.

Referential Integrity Check

We discussed the Operations sub-page and its Table maintenance section in Chapter 10. Now that we have defined a relation for the authors table (a non-InnoDB table), a new choice appears for the books table: Check referential integrity:

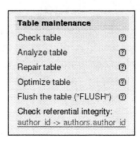

A link (here, author_id -> authors.author_id) appears for each defined relation, and clicking it starts a verification. For each row, the presence of the corresponding key in the foreign table is verified and the errors are reported. If the resulting page reports zero rows, this is good news!

This operation exists because for non-InnoDB tables, MySQL does not enforce referential integrity, and neither does phpMyAdmin. It is perfectly possible, for example, to import data in the books table, with invalid values for author_id.

Automatic Update of Metadata

phpMyAdmin keeps the metadata for internal relations synchronized with every change that is made to the tables. For example, renaming a column that is part of a relation would make phpMyAdmin rename it also in the metadata for its relations. The same thing happens when a column or a table is dropped.

Column-Commenting

MySQL 4 structure supports adding comments to a table, but not to a column. In Relation view, this feature is possible, thanks to phpMyAdmin's metadata.

	Comments
isbn	book number
title	
page_count	approximate
author_id	see authors table
language	
description	
cover_photo	
genre	
date_published	
	Go

These comments appear at various places—for example, in the export file (see Chapter 7), on the PDF relational schema (see Chapter 15), and in the Browse mode:

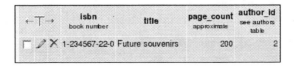

←T→	isbn book number	title	page_count approximate	author_id see authors table
☐ ✎ ✗	1-234567-22-0	Future souvenirs	200	2

Summary

In this chapter:

- We covered the installation of the necessary infrastructure for keeping special metadata (data about tables).
- We learned how to define relations between tables, both for InnoDB and non-InnoDB tables.
- We examined the modified behavior of phpMyAdmin when relations are present: choosing foreign keys, getting information from the foreign table, and column-commenting.

12

Entering SQL Commands

This chapter explains how we can enter our own SQL commands (queries) into phpMyAdmin and how we can keep a history of those queries.

SQL Query Box

phpMyAdmin allows us to accomplish many database operations via its graphical interface, but sometimes we have to rely on SQL query input to achieve complex operations. Here are examples of complex queries:

```
select department, avg(salary) from employees group by department
having years_experience > 10;
```

```
select from_days(to_days(curdate()) +30);
```

The query box is available from a number of places within phpMyAdmin.

Database View

We encounter our first query box when going to the SQL menu available in the Database view. This box is simple: we type in it some valid (hopefully) MySQL statement and click Go. In Chapter 8, we have already seen how to import query files from this panel.

For a default query to appear in this box, we can set it with the $cfg['DefaultQueryDatabase'] configuration directive, which is empty by default. We could put a query like SHOW TABLES FROM %d in this directive. The %d parameter in this query would be replaced by the current database name, resulting in SHOW TABLES FROM `dbbook` in the query box.

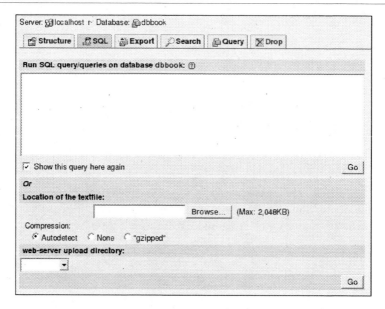

Table View

A slightly different box is available in the Table view.

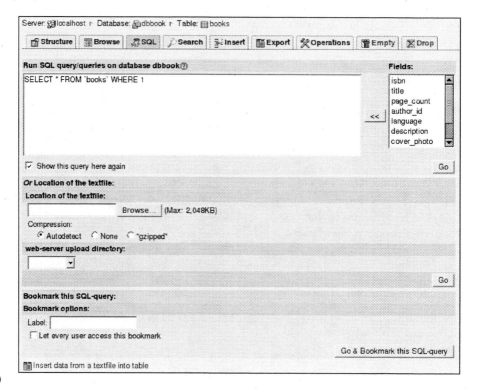

Accessed from either the SQL menu or the Structure menu, the query box is offered at two places based on the feedback received by the phpMyAdmin development team—the previous screenshot is the result of accessing the query box from the SQL menu. Some users prefer to have it on the same page as the complete structure; some prefer a page that does not display the whole structure because their tables have lots of columns and are slower to display, especially on slow Internet links. The lower part has bookmark-related choices (explained in Chapter 14). There is also a Fields selector and an Insert button on the right. The box already has a default query.

This query (SELECT * FROM `books` WHERE 1) is generated from the $cfg['DefaultQueryTable'] configuration directive, which contains SELECT * FROM %t WHERE 1. Here, the %t is replaced by the current table name. Another placeholder available in $cfg['DefaultQueryTable'] is %f, which would be replaced by the complete field list of this table, thus producing the query SELECT `isbn`, `title`, `page_count`, `author_id`, `language`, `description`, `cover_photo`, `genre` FROM `books` WHERE 1.

WHERE 1 is a condition that is always true, so the query can be executed as is. We can replace 1 with the exact condition we want or type a completely different query.

Fields Selector

The Fields selector is a way to speed up query entering. By choosing a field and clicking on the arrows <<, this field name is copied *at the current cursor position* in the query box. Here we select the author_id field, we remove the digit 1 and click <<. Then we add the condition = 2.

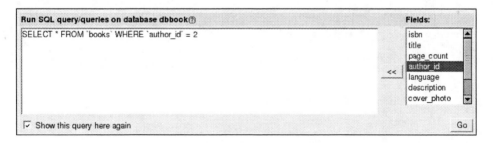

The Show this query here again option (checked by default) means that the query will stay in the box after its execution, if we are still on the same page. This can be better seen for a query like an UPDATE or DELETE, which affects a table but does not produce a separate results page.

Clicking Into the Query Box

The default value of the $cfg['TextareaAutoSelect'] configuration directive is TRUE. This is why the first click into this box selects all its contents (this is a way to quickly copy the contents elsewhere or delete it from the box).

The next click puts the cursor at the click position. If the directive is set to FALSE, the first click does not select all the contents of this text area.

Query Window

In Chapter 3, we discussed the purpose of this window, and the procedure to change some parameters (like dimension). This window can be easily opened from the left panel using the SQL icon or the Query window link, and is very convenient for entering a query and testing it:

The following shows the query window that appears over the right panel:

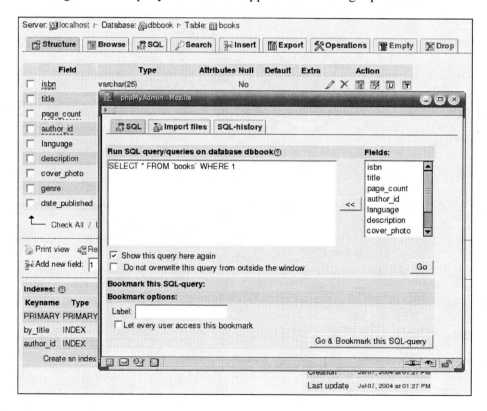

It contains the same Fields selector and << button used in a Table view context.

This distinct query window only appears if $cfg['QueryFrameJS'] is set to TRUE; we need to use a JavaScript-enabled browser. If this is set to FALSE, following the Query window link will only jump to the normal SQL page with the query box.

Query Window Options

The SQL tab is the default active tab in this window. This comes from the configuration directive $cfg['QueryWindowDefTab'], which contains sql by default. If we want another tab to be the default active tab, we can replace sql with files or history. Another value, full, shows the contents of all the three tabs at once.

In the query window, we see a checkbox for the Do not overwrite this query from outside the window choice. Normally this is not checked, and the changes we make while navigating and doing queries are reflected in the query window (this is called **synchronization**). For example, choosing a different database or table from the left or right panel would update the query window accordingly. But if we start to type a query directly in this window, the checkbox will get checked in order to protect its contents and remove synchronization. This way, the query composed here will be locked and protected.

JavaScript-Based SQL History

This feature collects all the *successful* SQL queries we execute, and modifies the Query window to make them available. If we close the window, they will be lost. This default type of history is temporary—$cfg['QueryHistoryDB'] is set to FALSE by default.

JavaScript-based history works in Opera, Mozilla-based browsers, and Internet Explorer.

Database-Based SQL History (Permanent)

Since we installed the linked-tables infrastructure (see Chapter 11), a more powerful history mechanism is available and is triggered by setting $cfg['QueryHistoryDB'] to TRUE.

After we try some queries from the query box, a history is built:

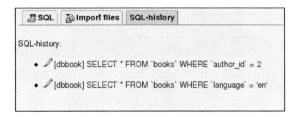

We see (in the reverse order) the last successful queries and the database on which they were made. Only the query types from the query box are kept in this history, not queries generated by phpMyAdmin itself (for example, by clicking on Browse). They are clickable for immediate execution, and the Edit icon is available to bring a recorded query in the query box for editing.

How many queries will be kept is controlled by $cfg['QueryHistoryMax'], which is set to 25 by default. This limit is not kept for performance reasons, but instead as a practical limit to achieve a visually unencumbered view. Extra queries are eliminated at login time in a process traditionally called **garbage collection**. The queries are stored in the table configured in $cfg['Servers'][$i]['history'].

Editing Query and Query Window

On the results page of a successful query, a header containing the executed query appears:

> **Showing rows 0 - 0 (1 total, Query took 0.0015 sec)**
>
> **SQL-query:**
> SELECT *
> FROM `books`
> WHERE `author_id` =2 LIMIT 0 , 30
>
> [Edit] [Explain SQL] [Create PHP Code] [Refresh]

Clicking Edit opens the Query window's SQL tab, with this query ready to be modified.

Multi-Statement Queries

In PHP/MySQL programming, we can only send one query at a time using the mysql_query() function call. phpMyAdmin allows for sending many queries in one transmission, using a semicolon as a separator. Suppose we type the following query in the query box:

```
insert into authors values (100,'Paul Smith','111-2222');
insert into authors values (101,'Melanie Smith','222-3333');
update authors set phone='444-5555' where author_name like '%Smith%';
```

We will receive the following results screen:

> **Your SQL-query has been executed successfully**
>
> **SQL-query:**
> INSERT INTO authors
> VALUES (100, 'Paul Smith', '111-2222') ;# Affected rows:1
> INSERT INTO authors
> VALUES (101, 'Melanie Smith', '222-3333') ;# Affected rows:1
> UPDATE authors SET phone = '444-5555' WHERE author_name LIKE '%Smith%';# Affected rows:3

We see the number of affected rows through comments because $cfg['VerboseMultiSubmit']$ is set to TRUE.

Let's send the same list of queries again, and watch the results:

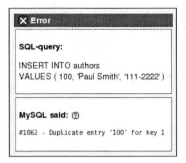

It is normal to receive a Duplicate entry error: the value 100 already exists. But what happens to the next INSERT statement? Execution stops at the first error because $cfg['IgnoreMultiSubmitErrors']$ is set to FALSE, telling phpMyAdmin to *not* ignore errors in multiple statements. If it is set to TRUE, the program successively tries all statements, and we get:

> **Your SQL-query has been executed successfully**
>
> **SQL-query:**
> INSERT INTO authors
> VALUES (100, 'Paul Smith', '111-2222') ;# Error
> INSERT INTO authors
> VALUES (101, 'Melanie Smith', '222-3333') ;# Error
> UPDATE authors SET phone = '444-5555' WHERE author_name LIKE '%Smith%';# MySQL returned an empty result set (i.e. zero rows).

This feature would not work as expected if we tried more than one SELECT statement. We would see only the results of the last SELECT.

Pretty Printing (Syntax-Highlighting)

By default, phpMyAdmin parses and highlights the various elements of any MySQL statement it processes. This is controlled by $cfg['SQP']['fmtType']$ set to 'html' by default. This mode uses a specific color for each different element (a reserved word, a variable, a comment, etc.), as described in the $cfg['SQP']['fmtColor']$ array— located in the theme-specific layout.inc.php. The default values are:

```
$cfg['SQP']['fmtColor']      = array(
    'comment'                => '#808000',
    'comment_mysql'          => '',
    'comment_ansi'           => '',
    'comment_c'              => '',
    'digit'                  => '',
    'digit_hex'              => 'teal',
```

```
        'digit_integer'        => 'teal',
        'digit_float'          => 'aqua',
        'punct'                => 'fuchsia',
        'alpha'                => '',
        'alpha_columnType'     => '#FF9900',
        'alpha_columnAttrib'   => '#0000FF',
        'alpha_reservedWord'   => '#990099',
        'alpha_functionName'   => '#FF0000',
        'alpha_identifier'     => 'black',
        'alpha_variable'       => '#800000',
        'quote'                => '#008000',
        'quote_double'         => '',
        'quote_single'         => '',
        'quote_backtick'       => ''
    );
```

In the previous examples, fmtType was set to 'text', because this mode is more legible in a book. This mode inserts line breaks at logical points inside a MySQL statement, but there is no color involved. With fmtType set to 'html', phpMyAdmin would report the SQL statements as:

```
SQL-query:
INSERT INTO authors
VALUES ( 100, 'Paul Smith', '111-2222' ) ; # Error
INSERT INTO authors
VALUES ( 101, 'Melanie Smith', '222-3333' ) ; # Error
UPDATE authors SET phone = '444-5555' WHERE author_name LIKE '%Smith%'; # MySQL returned an empty result set (i.e. zero rows).
```

fmtType set to 'none' removes every kind of formatting, leaving our syntax intact:

```
SQL-query:
insert into authors values (100, 'Paul Smith', '111-2222'); # Error
insert into authors values (101, 'Melanie Smith', '222-3333'); # Error
update authors set phone='444-5555' where author_name like '%Smith%'; # MySQL returned an empty result set (i.e. zero rows).
```

The multi-dimensional arrays used for holding some parameters in the configuration file reflect a programming style adopted by the phpMyAdmin development team. This avoids having very long parameter names.

SQL Validator

Each time phpMyAdmin transmits a query, the MySQL server interprets it and provides feedback. The syntax of the query must follow MySQL rules, which are not the same as standard SQL. Conforming to standard SQL ensures that our queries may be used on other SQL implementations.

A free external service—the Mimer SQL Validator—is offered. It's available directly from phpMyAdmin and validates our query according to Core SQL-99 rules, and gives a report. The Validator's home page is located at
http://developer.mimer.com/validator/index.htm.

This service stores anonymously the queries it receives, for statistical purposes. When storing the queries, it replaces database, table, and columns names with generic names. Strings and numbers that are part of the query are replaced with generic values so as to protect the original information.

System Requirements

This Validator is available as a SOAP service. Our PHP server must have XML, PCRE, and PEAR support. We need some PEAR modules too. The following command (executed on the server by the system administrator) installs the modules we need:

```
pear install Net_Socket Net_URL HTTP_Request Mail_Mime Net_DIME SOAP
```

If we have problems with this command due to some of the modules being in a beta state, we can execute the following command, which installs SOAP and other dependent modules:

```
pear -d preferred_state=beta install -a SOAP
```

Making the Validator Available

Some parameters must be configured in config.inc.php. Setting $cfg['SQLQuery']['validate'] to TRUE enables the Validate SQL link.

We also have to enable the Validator itself (as other validators might be available on future phpMyAdmin versions). This is done by setting $cfg['SQLValidator']['use'] to TRUE.

The Validator is accessed with an anonymous Validator account by default, as configured by the following:

```
$cfg['SQLValidator']['username'] = '';
$cfg['SQLValidator']['password'] = '';
```

If the company has provided us with an account, we can instead use that account information here.

Validator Results

There are two kinds of reports returned by the Validator: one if the query conforms to the standard, and another if it does not.

Standard-Conforming Queries

We will try a simple query: select * from books. We enter this query in the query box as usual and send it. On the results page, we now see an additional link: Validate SQL.:

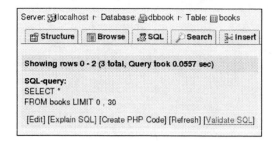

Clicking on Validate SQL produces the following report:

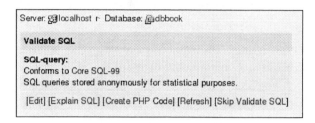

We have the option to click Skip Validate SQL to see our original query.

Non Standard-Conforming Queries

Let's try this query, which works correctly in MySQL: `select * from books where language = 'en'`. Sending it to the Validator produces the following report:

```
Validate SQL

SQL-query:
select * from books where {error: 1}language = 'en'

Errors:

    1.  syntax error: language
            expected: { + - : ? <ascii identifier> <character set identifier>
                    <decimal literal> <delimited identifier> <float literal>
                    <hex string literal> <identifier> <integer literal>
                    <national string literal> <string literal> ANY ARRAY CASE CAST
                    CURRENT_DATE CURRENT_DEFAULT_TRANSFORM_GROUP CURRENT_PATH
                    CURRENT_ROLE CURRENT_TIME CURRENT_TIMESTAMP
                    CURRENT_TRANSFORM_GROUP_FOR_TYPE CURRENT_USER DATE DEREF EXISTS
                    FALSE GROUPING INTERVAL LOCALTIME LOCALTIMESTAMP MODULE NEW NOT
                    REPEAT ROW SESSION_USER SOME SYSTEM_USER TIME TIMESTAMP TREAT
                    TRUE UNIQUE UNKNOWN USER VALUE
            correction: <identifier>

SQL queries stored anonymously for statistical purposes.

                [Edit] [Explain SQL] [Create PHP Code] [Refresh] [Skip Validate SQL]
```

Each time the Validator finds a problem, it adds a message like {error: 1} at the point of error, and a footnote in the report. This time, the language column name is non-standard, so the Validator tells us that it was expecting an identifier at this point.

Another case is that of the backquotes. If we just click on Browse for table books, phpMyAdmin generates select * from `books`, enclosing the table name with backquotes. This is the MySQL way of protecting identifiers, which might contain special characters, like spaces or international characters, or reserved words. However, sending this query to the Validator shows us that the backquotes do not conform to standard SQL. We even get two errors—one for each backquote:

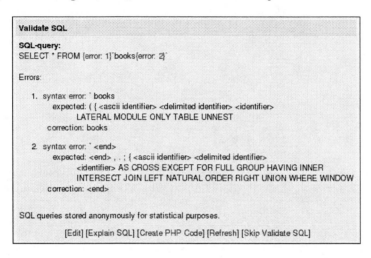

Summary

This chapter covered:

- The purpose of query boxes
- Where we can find them
- How to use the field selector
- Some query window options
- How to get a history of the typed commands
- Multi-statement queries
- Using the SQL Validator

13

Multi-Table Query Generator

The Search pages in the Database or Table view are intended for single-table lookups. This chapter covers the multi-table **Query by example (QBE)** feature available in the Database view.

Many phpMyAdmin users work in the Table view, table by table, and thus tend to overlook the multi-table query generator, which is a wonderful feature for fine-tuning queries. To open the page for this feature, we go to the Database view for a specific database (the query generator supports working on only one database at a time) and click on Query.

The query generator is not only useful in multi-table situations, but also for a single table. It enables us to specify multiple criteria for a column, a feature that the Search page in Table view does not possess.

> The examples in this chapter assume that a single-user installation of the linked-tables infrastructure has been made—see Chapter 11—thus producing more tables in the dbbook database.

The screenshot overleaf shows the initial QBE page. It contains the following elements:

- Criteria columns
- An interface to add criteria rows
- An interface to add criteria columns
- A table selector
- The query area
- Buttons to update or to execute the query

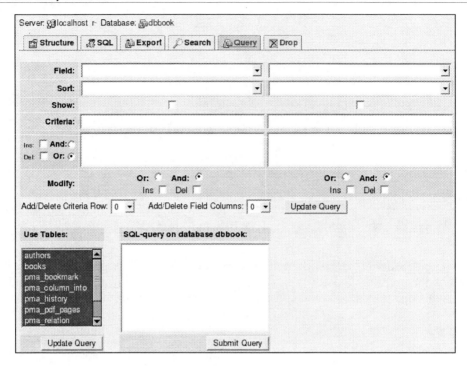

Choosing Tables

The initial selection includes all the tables. Consequently, the Field selector contains a great number of fields. For our example, we will work only with the authors and books tables:

We then click Update Query. This refreshes the screen and reduces the number of fields available in the Field selector. We can always change the table choice later, using our browser's mechanism for multiple choices in drop-down menus (usually control-click).

Column Criteria

Three criteria columns are provided by default. This section discusses the options we have for editing their criteria, which include options for selecting fields, sorting individual columns, entering conditions for individual columns, etc.

Field Selector: Single-Column or All Columns

The Field selector contains all individual columns for the selected tables, *plus* a special choice ending with an asterisk (*) for each table, which means 'all the fields' are selected:

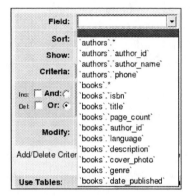

To display all fields from the authors table, we choose `authors`.* and we just check the Show checkbox, entering no Sort and no Criteria. In our case, we select `authors`.`author_name` since we want to enter some criteria for the author's name.

Sort

For each selected individual column, we can specify a sort (in Ascending or Descending order) or let this line remain intact (meaning no sort). If we choose more than one sorted column, the sort will be done with a priority from left to right.

> If we ask to sort a column, we should also click to Show it.

Show

We choose Show to see the column in the results. Sometimes, we may just want to apply a criterion on a column and not include it in the resulting page. Here we add the phone field, ask for a sort on it, and choose to show both the name and phone number. We also ask a sort on the name in ascending order. The sort will be done first by name, and then by phone number if the names are identical. This is because the name is in a column criterion to the left of the phone column and thus has a higher priority:

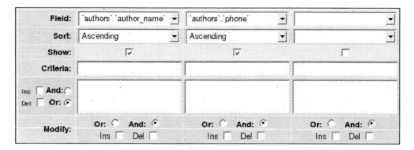

Updating the Query

At any point, we can click the Update Query button to see the progress of our generated query. We surely have to click it at least once before executing the query. For now, let's click it and see the query generated in the query area. In the following examples, we will click Update Query after each modification:

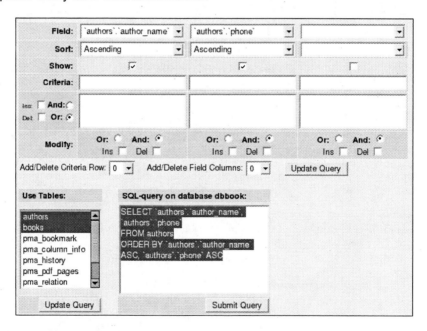

We have selected two tables, but have not chosen any columns from the books table yet. So, this table is not mentioned in the generated query.

Criteria

In the Criteria line, we can enter a condition (respecting the SQL WHERE clause's syntax) for each of the corresponding columns. By default, we have two criteria rows. To find all authors with Smith in their name, we use a LIKE criterion and click Update Query:

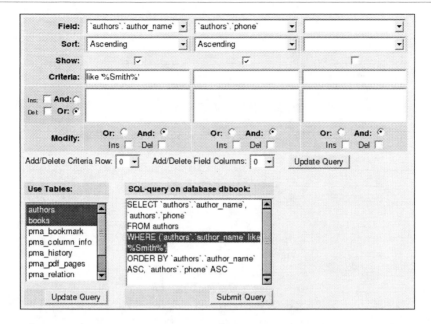

We have another line available to enter an additional criterion. Let's say we want to find the author 'Maria Sunshine' as well. This time, we use an = condition. The two condition rows will be joined by an OR selected by default on the left side of the interface:

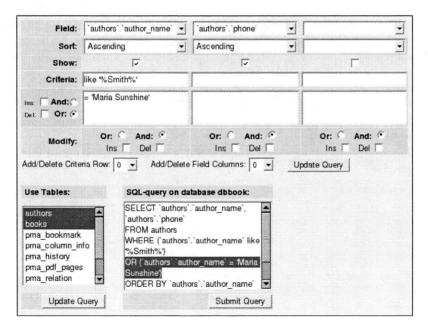

To better demonstrate that the OR condition links both the criteria rows, let's now add a condition on the phone number:

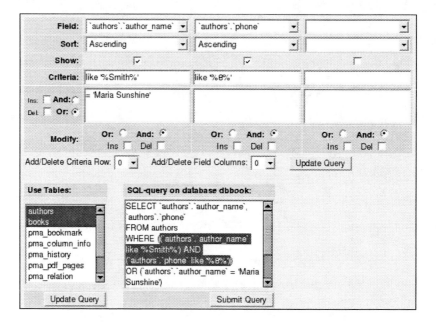

By examining the positioning of the AND and OR operators, we can see that the first conditions are linked by a AND (because AND is chosen under the author_name column) and that the second row of conditions is linked by an OR with the rest. The condition we just added (like '%8%') is not meant to find anyone, since in an exercise in Chapter 12 we changed the phone number of all authors with name 'Smith' to '444-5555'.

If we want another criterion on the same column, we just add a criteria row.

Adjusting the Number of Criteria Rows

The number of criteria rows can be changed in two ways. First, we can select the Ins checkbox under Criteria to add one criteria row (which is done after an Update Query):

We can also use the Add/Delete Criteria Row dialog; here we choose to add two rows:

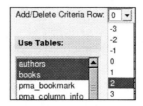

This produces the following:

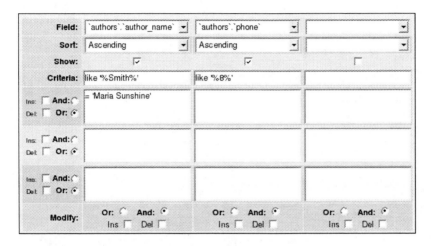

We can also remove criteria rows. This can be done by choosing negative numbers in the Add/Delete Criteria Row dialog or by ticking the Del checkbox beside the row(s) we want to remove. Let's remove the two rows we just added since we don't need them now:

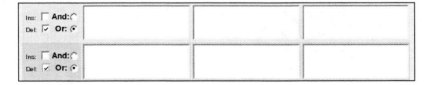

The Update query button refreshes the page with the specified adjustment.

Adjusting the Number of Criteria Columns

We can add or delete columns with a similar mechanism: the Ins or Del checkboxes under each column, or the Add/Delete Field Columns dialog. We already had one unused column. Here we have added one column, using the Ins checkbox located under the unused column (this time we will need it):

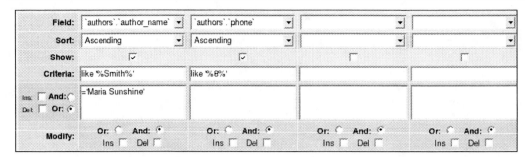

Automatic Joins

Let's now add some fields from our books table and see what happens:

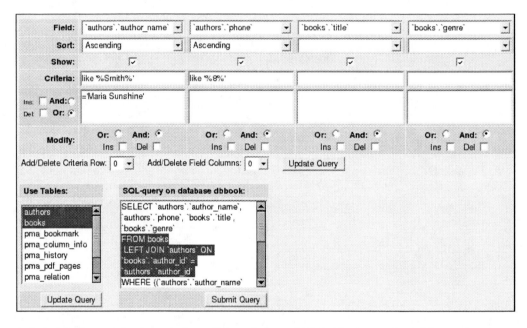

phpMyAdmin uses its knowledge of the relations defined between the tables, to generate a LEFT JOIN on the common author_id key field.

There may be more than two tables involved in a JOIN.

Executing the Query

Clicking the Submit Query button sends the query for execution. In the current phpMyAdmin version (2.6.0) there is no easy way (except by using the browser's Back button) to come back to the query generation page after we have submitted our query. The next chapter (*Bookmarks*) discusses how to save the generated query for later execution.

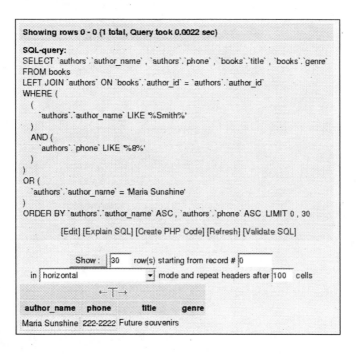

Summary

We have covered the following concepts:

- Opening the query generator
- Choosing the tables
- Entering column criteria
- Sorting and showing columns
- Altering the number of criteria rows or columns
- AND/OR relations between rows and columns
- Using automatic joins between tables

Bookmarks

This chapter covers one of the linked-tables features: query bookmarks. Being able to label queries and recall them by label can be a real time saver. In Chapter 12 we have learned about the SQL history feature, which automatically stores queries (temporarily or permanently).

Bookmarks are queries that are:

- Stored permanently
- Viewable
- Erasable
- Related to one database
- Recorded only as a consequence of a user's wish
- Labeled
- Private by default (only available to the user creating them), but possibly public

A bookmark can also have a variable part, as explained in the *Passing a Parameter Value to a Bookmark* section later in the chapter.

There is no bookmark sub-page to manage bookmarks. Instead, the various actions on bookmarks are available on specific pages such as results pages or query box pages.

Creating a Bookmark after a Successful Query

Initial bookmark creation is made possible by the Bookmark this SQL-query button. This button appears only after execution of a query that generates results (when at least one row is found), and so, this method for creating bookmarks only stores SELECT statements. For example, a complex query produced by the multi-table query generator (as seen in Chapter 13) could be stored as a bookmark this way, provided it finds results.

Let's see an example. In the Search page for the books table, we enter the search values as shown in the following screenshot:

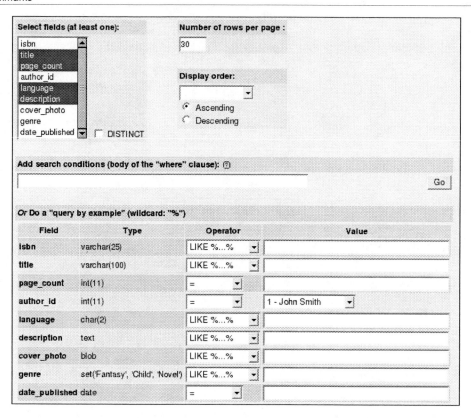

The results page has a bookmark dialog. We have to enter only a label for this bookmark and click Bookmark this SQL-query to save this query as a bookmark. Bookmarks are saved in the table defined by $cfg['Servers'][$i]['bookmarktable'].

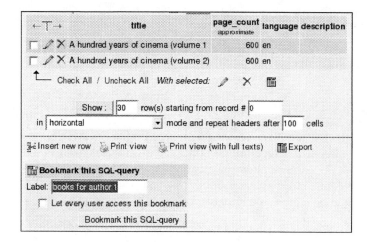

This bookmark dialog can be seen on any page that contains results. In fact, we could just click Browse for a table to get results and then store this query as a bookmark. However, it does not make much sense to store (in a bookmark) a query that can easily be made with one click.

Storing a Bookmark before Sending a Query

Sometimes we may want to store a bookmark even if a query does not find any results. This may be the case if the matching data is not yet present or the query is not a SELECT. To achieve this, we have the Go & Bookmark this SQL-query dialog available as follows:

- The Table view: on each page where a query box is displayed
- The query window: the SQL tab

We now go to the SQL sub-page of the books table, enter a query, and directly put the books in French bookmark label in the Bookmark options Label field. Then, instead of clicking Go to execute the query, we click Go & Bookmark this SQL-query, which executes and stores the query. It does not matter if the query finds nothing:

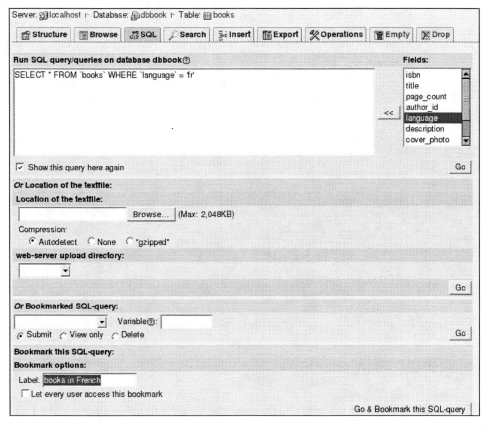

This is how we can generate bookmarks for non-SELECT queries like UPDATE, DELETE, CREATE TABLE, and so on.

Multi-Query Bookmarks

A single bookmark can also store more than one query (separated by a semicolon). This is mostly useful for non-SELECT queries. Stacking a lot of SELECTs would not yield the intended result because we only see the data fetched by the last SELECT.

Recalling from the Bookmarks List

These bookmarks can now be easily found on the following pages:

- The Table view: Structure or SQL sub-page of any table from dbbook
- The query window: the SQL-History tab
- While browsing the pma_bookmark table (see the *Executing Bookmarks from pma_bookmark* section later)
- The Database view: SQL sub-page of the dbbook database

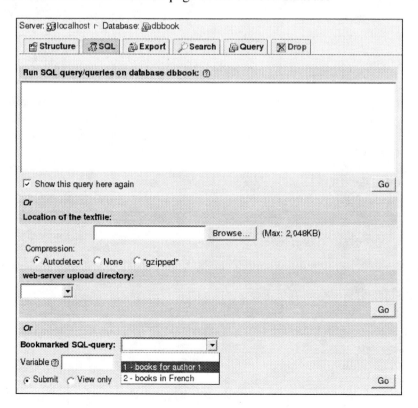

Bookmarks are numbered by the system. Three choices are available when recalling a bookmark: Submit, View only, and Delete (Submit being the default).

Bookmark Execution

Choosing the first bookmark and hitting Go executes the stored query and displays its results. The page resulting from a bookmark execution does not have another dialog to create a bookmark as this would be superfluous.

> The results we get are not necessarily the same as when we created the bookmark. They reflect the current contents of the database. Only the query is stored as a bookmark.

Bookmark Manipulation

Sometimes we may just want to ascertain the contents of a bookmark. Here we choose the second bookmark and select View only:

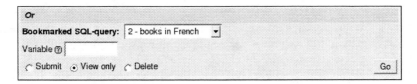

The query will only be displayed. We could then click Edit and rework its contents. By doing so, we would be editing a copy of the original bookmarked query. To keep this new edited query, we can save it as a bookmark, but this will create another bookmark *even if we choose the same bookmark label*. Bookmarks carry an identifying number as well as a user-chosen label.

A bookmark can be erased with the Delete option. There is *no* confirmation dialog to confirm the deletion of the bookmark. Deletion is followed only by a message stating The bookmark has been deleted.

Public Bookmarks

All bookmarks we create are private by default. When a bookmark is created, the user we are logged in as is stored with the bookmark. Suppose we choose Let every user access this bookmark as shown in the following screenshot:

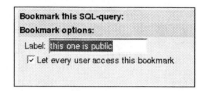

This would have the following effect:

- All users that have access to the same database (the current one) will have access to the bookmark.

- The users' ability to see meaningful results from the bookmark depends on the privileges they have on the tables referenced in the bookmark.

- The users will be able to delete the bookmark.

Default Initial Query for a Table

In the previous examples, we chose bookmark labels according to our preferences, but by convention, if a bookmark has the same name as a table, it will be executed when Browse is clicked for this table.

Suppose we are interested in viewing (by default, in the Browse mode) the books with a page count lower than 300. We first generate the appropriate query, and then on the results page we use books as a label:

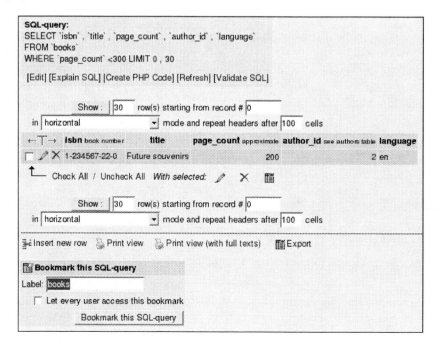

Bookmark Parameters

If we look again at the first bookmark we created (finding all books for author 1), we realize that, although useful, it was limited to always finding the same author.

A special query syntax enables the passing of parameters to bookmarks. This syntax uses the fact that SQL comments enclosed within /* and */ are ignored by MySQL. If the /*[VARIABLE]*/ construct exists somewhere in the query, it will be expanded at execution time with the value provided when recalling the bookmark.

Creating a Parameterized Bookmark

Let's say we want to find all books for a given author when we know the author's name. We first enter the query as shown in the following screenshot. Note that the part between the comments characters (/* */) will be expanded later, and the tags removed:

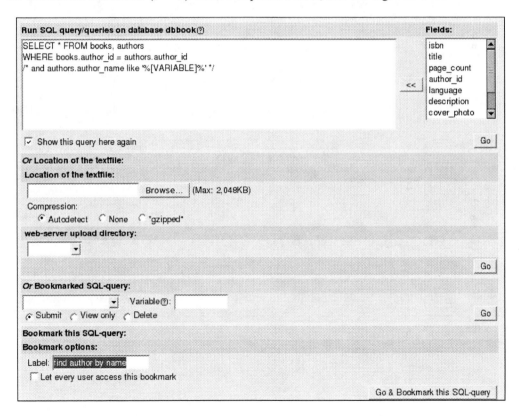

We label it and click Go & Bookmark this SQL-query. The first execution of the query does nothing special, and stores the bookmark.

In this example, we have two conditions in the WHERE clause, of which one contains the special syntax. If our only criterion in the WHERE clause needed a parameter, we could use a syntax like WHERE 1 /* and author_id = [VARIABLE] */.

Passing a Parameter Value to a Bookmark

To test the bookmark, we recall it as usual and enter a value in the Variable field:

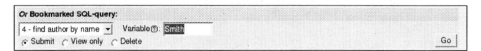

When we click Go, we see the expanded query and author Smith's books:

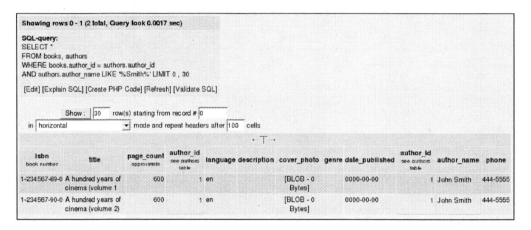

Executing Bookmarks from pma_bookmark

This feature is only available to users who have access to the pma_bookmark table. This is the default name given when the linked-tables infrastructure is installed. In a multi-user installation, this table is usually located in a database invisible to unprivileged users. Browsing this table displays a new Execute bookmarked query button, which triggers the execution of the query:

Summary

In this chapter:

- We saw how to record bookmarks (after or before sending a query) and then manipulate them. We then saw that some bookmarks can be made public.

- We covered the notions of the default initial query for Browse mode, passing parameters to bookmarks, and executing them directly from browsing the pma_bookmark table.

15

System Documentation

Producing and maintaining good documentation about data structure is crucial for a project's success, especially when it's a team project. Fortunately, phpMyAdmin has features that take care of this. When phpMyAdmin generates results, there is always a Print view link that can be used to generate a printable report of the data. The Print view feature can also be used to produce basic documentation, and is done in two steps. The first click on Print view puts a report on screen, with a Print button at end of the page. This Print button generates a report formatted for the printer.

Database Print View

On the Structure sub-page of a database, Print view generates the list of tables and is suitable to see the size of tables, number of records, table comments, and the date.

Server: localhost ► Database: dbbook

Table	Records	Type	Size	Comments	
authors	4	MyISAM	2.1 KB	Creation:	Jul 07, 2004 at 01:28 PM
				Last update:	Jul 07, 2004 at 02:56 PM
books	3	MyISAM	8.5 KB	Creation:	Jul 07, 2004 at 01:27 PM
				Last update:	Jul 07, 2004 at 01:27 PM
pma_bookmark	0	MyISAM	1.0 KB	Bookmarks Creation:	Jul 08, 2004 at 08:58 AM
				Last update:	Jul 08, 2004 at 08:58 AM
pma_column_info	0	MyISAM	1.0 KB	Column information for phpMyAdmin Creation:	Jul 08, 2004 at 08:58 AM
				Last update:	Jul 08, 2004 at 08:58 AM
pma_history	0	MyISAM	1.0 KB	SQL history for phpMyAdmin Creation:	Jul 08, 2004 at 08:58 AM
				Last update:	Jul 08, 2004 at 08:58 AM
pma_pdf_pages	0	MyISAM	1.0 KB	PDF relation pages for phpMyAdmin Creation:	Jul 08, 2004 at 08:58 AM
				Last update:	Jul 08, 2004 at 08:58 AM
pma_relation	0	MyISAM	1.0 KB	Relation table Creation:	Jul 08, 2004 at 08:58 AM
				Last update:	Jul 08, 2004 at 08:58 AM
pma_table_coords	0	MyISAM	1.0 KB	Table coordinates for phpMyAdmin PDF output Creation:	Jul 08, 2004 at 08:58 AM
				Last update:	Jul 08, 2004 at 08:58 AM
pma_table_info	0	MyISAM	1.0 KB	Table information for phpMyAdmin Creation:	Jul 08, 2004 at 08:58 AM
				Last update:	Jul 08, 2004 at 08:58 AM
9 table(s)	7	–	17.6 KB		

Print

Selective Database Print View

Sometimes we prefer to get a report for only certain tables. This is possible from the Structure sub-page of a database, by choosing the tables we want and using the drop-down menu Print view:

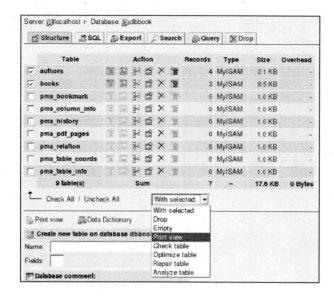

Table Print View

There is a Print view link even on the Structure sub-page of every table, and this produces information about columns, indexes, space usage, and row statistics, as shown:

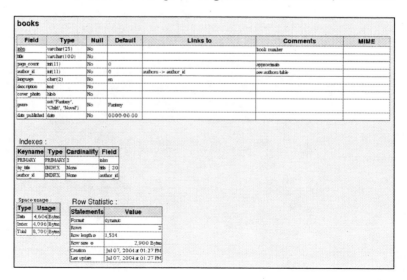

Data Dictionary

A more complete report about tables and columns for a database is available in the Database view, from the Structure sub-page. We just have to click Data dictionary to get a report about all tables (shown partially here):

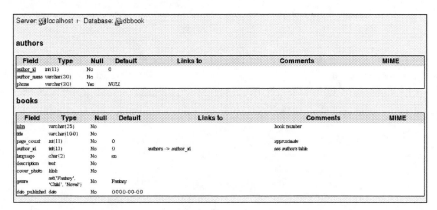

The MIME column is empty until we add MIME-related information to some columns; this is explained in Chapter 16.

Relational Schema in PDF

In Chapter 11, we defined relations between the books and authors tables. These relations were used for various foreign key functions (for example, getting a list of possible values in Insert mode). Now we will examine a feature that enables us to generate a custom-made relational schema for our tables in the popular PDF format.

Adding a Third Table to Our Model

To get a more complete schema, we now add another table to our database, the countries table. Here is the export file:

```
CREATE TABLE `countries` (
  `country_code` char(2) NOT NULL default '',
  `description` varchar(50) NOT NULL default '',
  PRIMARY KEY  (`country_code`)
) TYPE=MyISAM;

INSERT INTO `countries` VALUES ('ca', 'Canada');
INSERT INTO `countries` VALUES ('uk', 'United Kingdom');
```

We will now link this table to the authors table. First, in Relation view for the countries table, we specify the Field to display:

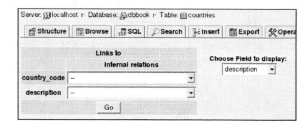

Then, on the authors table, we add the same field country_code, and in Relation view, we link it to the newly created countries table. We must remember to click Go for the relation to be recorded. For this example, it is not necessary to enter any country data for an author, as we are interested only in the relational schema.

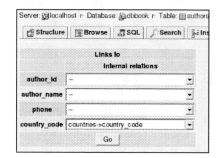

Edit PDF Pages

In the Database view for the dbbook database, we go to the Structure sub-page and click Edit PDF pages. Each relational schema is called a page, and here we can create or edit them.

Page Planning

In the current phpMyAdmin version, a relational schema cannot span multiple databases. But even working with just one database, the number of tables might be large. Representing the various relations between them in a clear way could be a challenge. This is why we may use many pages, each showing some tables and their relations.

We must also take into account the dimensions of the final output. Printing on letter-size paper gives us less space to show all our tables and still have a legible schema.

Create a New Page

Since there are no existing pages, we need to create one. Since our most important table is about books, we choose to name this page books.

In the next step, we will choose which tables we wish to see on the relational schema. We could choose each table one by one, but for a good start, it is recommended to select the Automatic layout checkbox. This option takes all the related tables from our database and puts them on the list of tables to be included on the schema. It then generates appropriate coordinates so that the tables will appear in a spiral layout, starting from the center of the schema. Those coordinates are expressed in millimeters, with (0,0) being located at the upper left corner. We then click Go.

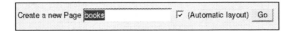

Edit a Page

We now get a page with three different sections. The first one is the master menu, where we choose the page on which we want to work (from the drop-down menu); we can also Delete the chosen page. We also could eventually create a second schema (page).

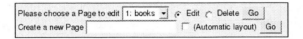

The next section is the table placement part. We now see the benefit of the Automatic layout feature: we already have our three tables selected, with (X,Y) coordinates filled. We have the option to add a table (on the last line), delete a table (using the checkbox), and change the coordinates (they represent the position of the upper left corner of each table on the schema):

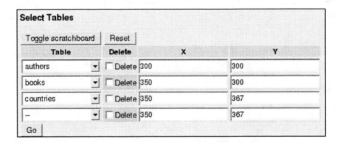

To help set exact coordinates, a visual editor is available for JavaScript-enabled browsers. This editor appears on clicking the Toggle scratchboard button once, and will disappear on clicking this button again. On the scratchboard, we can move tables at will via drag and drop, and watch the coordinates change accordingly. The representation of tables seen on the scratchboard is only a rough estimate, compared to the final PDF output.

When we are satisfied with the layout, we must click Go to save it.

Display a Page

The last section of the screen is the PDF report generation dialog. This section is also available in the Database view on the Structure sub-page, now that we have created at least one page definition:

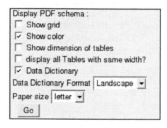

The available options are:

- Show grid: The schema will have a grid layer, with coordinates displayed.

- Show color: The links between tables, table names, and special columns (primary keys and display fields) will be in color.

- Show dimensions of table: This displays the visual dimension of each table in the table title, for example 32x30.

- Display all Tables with same width? Normally, the width adjusts itself according to the table and column names; same width uses the width of the largest table for all other tables. This can improve the visual result.

- Data Dictionary: This is the data dictionary that was covered in this chapter; this setting includes it at beginning of the report.

- Data Dictionary format: Here we choose the printed orientation of the dictionary.

- Paper size: Changing this will influence the schema and the scratchboard dimensions.

In `config.inc.php`, the following parameters define the available paper sizes and the default choice:

```
$cfg['PDFPageSizes']        = array('A3', 'A4', 'A5', 'letter',
'legal');
$cfg['PDFDefaultPageSize']  = 'A4';
```

The following screenshot shows the last page of the generated report (the schema page) in the PDF format. The first four pages contain the data dictionary, with an additional feature: on each page, the table name is clickable to reach the schema, and in the schema, each table is clickable to reach the corresponding page in the data dictionary.

Arrows point in the direction of the corresponding foreign table and each relation line uses a specific color to characterize each relation. If the Show color option has been selected, primary keys are shown in red, and display fields in blue:

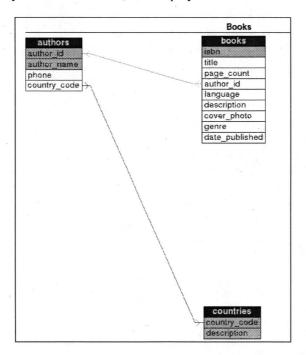

Another example generated from the same books PDF page definition, with the grid and no color is shown in the following screenshot:

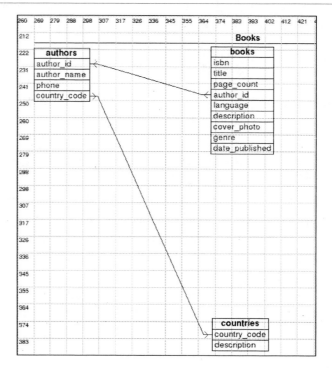

Note about Fonts Used

In the PDF schema, all the text we see is drawn using a specific font. phpMyAdmin tries to use the first font defined in the current language's message file (for example, lang/english-iso-8859-1.inc.php) according to the configuration directive $right_font_family, which contains 'arial, helvetica, geneva, sans-serif'. However, not all font families are supported.

For actual PDF generation, phpMyAdmin relies on the fpdf library (http://www.fpdf.org). This library has two ways of using fonts: embedded and not embedded. Embedded fonts would have produced a bigger PDF file, because the whole font would be included in the PDF. This is why the default option chosen by phpMyAdmin is not embedded.

For this to work, the library uses TrueType fonts present in the client operating system, and needs an interface to those fonts. The interface is contained in font mapping files, located in the libraries/fpdf/font directory.

The library can make some font substitutions, but in general, we should ensure that the necessary font mapping file is present. An example of substitution: for English, the first font defined in $right_font_family is arial and phpMyAdmin uses helvetica instead. Standard font mapping files shipped with phpMyAdmin are helvetica, courier, times, and tahoma.

To add a font mapping file, we must first add it to the library (as explained in a tutorial available on the `http://www.fpdf.org` website), and then modify phpMyAdmin's `pdf_schema.php` source code.

Summary

This chapter covered the documentation features offered by phpMyAdmin:

- Print view for a database or a table for a simple table or columns list
- Data dictionary for the complete column list
- PDF relational schema, including how to create and modify a PDF schema page and use the visual editor (scratchboard)

MIME-Based Transformations

Here we cover a powerful phpMyAdmin feature: its ability to transform a column's contents according to specific rules: the transformations. This chapter describes how we can transform the contents that we see in the Browse mode for a table. Normally, the exact contents of each row are displayed, except that:

- TEXT and character fields might be truncated, according to $cfg['LimitChars'] and whether we have clicked on the Full Text icon.
- BLOB fields might be replaced by a message like [BLOB - 1.5 KB].

We will use the term **cell** to indicate a specific column of a specific row. The cell containing the cover photo for the 'Future souvenirs' book (a BLOB column) is currently displayed as cryptic data like ‰PNG\r\n\Z\n\0\0\0\rIHDR\0 or as a message stating the BLOB's size. It would be interesting to see a thumbnail of the picture directly in phpMyAdmin, and possibly the picture itself.

We define **transformation** as a mechanism by which all the cells relating to a column are transformed at browse time, using the metadata defined for this column. Only the cells visible on the results page are transformed. The transformation logic itself is coded in PHP scripts, stored in libraries/transformations, and called using a plug-in architecture.

To enable this feature, we must set $cfg['BrowseMIME'] to TRUE in config.inc.php. The relational system must be in place (see Chapter 11), because the metadata necessary for the transformations is not available in the official MySQL table structure; it is an addition made especially for phpMyAdmin.

In the documentation section on phpMyAdmin's home site, there is a link pointing to additional information for developers who would like to learn the internal structure of the plug-ins in order to code their own transformations.

MIME Column's Settings

If we go to the Table view to the Structure page for the books table and click the Change link for the cover_photo, we see three additional attributes—such as the **Multimedia Internet Mail Extension (MIME)** type—for the field:

- MIME-type
- Browser transformation
- Transformation options

Comments	MIME-type	Browser transformation	Transformation options***
	▼	▼	

For a specific field, it is possible to indicate to phpMyAdmin only **one** type of transformation. Here, the field being a BLOB could hold any kind of data, but for phpMyAdmin to interpret and act correctly on the data, the transformation system must be informed of the data format and the intended results. Accordingly, we have to ensure that we upload data that always follows the same file format.

We will first learn the purpose of those attributes, and then try some possibilities in the *Examples of Transformation* section.

MIME Type

The MIME specification has been chosen as a metadata attribute to categorize the kind of data a column holds. The current possible values are:

- image/jpeg
- image/png
- text/plain

The auto-detect option in the menu is yet to be implemented, so we do not use it.

The text/plain type can be chosen for a column containing any kind of text—for example, XHTML or XML text.

Browser Transformations

This is where we set the exact transformation to be done. More than one transformation may be supported for one MIME type—for example, for the image/jpeg type, we have two transformations available: image/jpeg: inline for a clickable thumbnail of the image, and image/jpeg: link to display just a link.

As we can see on the following image, moving the mouse over each choice in the drop-down menu gives a short explanation of the corresponding transformation. A more complete explanation of the transformations and the possible options is available on clicking on the transformation descriptions link.

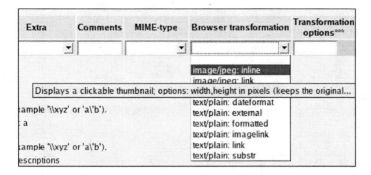

Transformation Options

We will see in the *Examples of Transformations* section that some transformations accept options. For example, a transformation that generates an image will need the width and height in pixels. A comma is used to separate the values in the option list, and some options may need to be enclosed within quotes.

Some options have a default value, and we must be careful to respect the documented order for options. For example, if there are two options and we only want to specify a value for the second option, we can use empty quotes as a placeholder for the first option to let the system use its default value.

Requirements for Image Generation

The normal generation of thumbnails requires that some components exist on the web server and that a parameter in config.inc.php be correctly configured.

GD2

phpMyAdmin uses internally some functions to create the thumbnails. Those functions need the GD2 library to be present in our PHP server.

phpMyAdmin can detect the presence of the correct GD2 library, but this detection takes some time, and takes place not once per session but almost *on every action taken* in phpMyAdmin.

The $cfg['GD2Available'] parameter in config.inc.php, with its default value of 'auto' indicates that a detection of the library presence and version is needed.

If we know that the GD2 library is available, execution will be quicker if we set $cfg['GD2Available'] to yes. If it is not available, it is recommended to put a no there.

JPEG and PNG Library

Our PHP server needs to have support for JPEG and PNG images if we or our users want to generate thumbnails for those types of images.

Memory

On some PHP servers, the default value in php.ini for memory_limit is 8 MB. This is too low for correct image manipulation. For example, in one test, a value of 11 MB in memory_limit was needed to generate the thumbnail from a 300 KB JPEG.

Examples of Transformations

We will now discuss a few transformation examples. We will start by changing the field type of our cover_photo field.

Clickable Thumbnail (.jpeg or .png)

We change our cover_photo field type from BLOB to MEDIUMBLOB to ensure we can upload photos that are bigger than 65 KB to it. We then enter the following attributes:

MIME-type	Browser transformation	Transformation options***
image/jpeg ▾	image/jpeg: inline ▾	100,80

Here, the options are presented as width,height. If we omit the options, the default values are 100,100. The thumbnail generation code preserves the original aspect ratio of the image, and so the values entered are the *maximum* width and height of the generated image. Then we upload a .jpeg file in a cell (using instructions from Chapter 6). As a result, we get the following in Browse mode for this table:

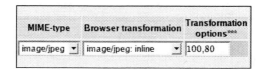

←T→	isbn book number	title	page_count approximate	author_id see authors table	language	description	cover_photo
☐ ✎ ✗	1-234567-22-0	Future souvenirs	200	2	en		
☐ ✎ ✗	1-234567-89-0	A hundred years of cinema (volume 1	600	1	en		[BLOB - 0 Bytes]
☐ ✎ ✗	1-234567-90-0	A hundred years of cinema (volume 2)	600	1	en		[BLOB - 0 Bytes]

↑ ⌐— Check All / Uncheck All *With selected:* ✎ ✗ ▤

This thumbnail can be clicked to reveal the full-size photo.

> The thumbnail is not stored anywhere in MySQL, but generated each time we go in Browse mode for this set of rows. On a Pentium-III 500 MHz server, we commonly experience a generation time of 0.5 to 1 second per image.

For a .png file, we have to use image/png as MIME type, and image/png: inline as the transformation.

Another point to note: the $cfg['ShowBlob'] parameter does not influence the thumbnail's display—it can be set to TRUE or FALSE.

Link to an Image

To get a link without thumbnails, we use the image/jpeg: link transformation. There are no transformation options. This link can then be used to view or download the photo (by right-clicking on the link):

←—T—→	isbn book number	title	page_count approximate	author_id see authors table	language	description	cover_photo
☐ ✎ ✕	1-234567-22-0	Future souvenirs	200	2	en		[BLOB]
☐ ✎ ✕	1-234567-89-0	A hundred years of cinema (volume 1	600	1	en		[BLOB]
☐ ✎ ✕	1-234567-90-0	A hundred years of cinema (volume 2)	600	1	en		[BLOB]

Check All / Uncheck All *With selected:* ✎ ✕ ▤

Date Formatting

We have a field named date_published in our books table; let's ensure that it's type is DATETIME. Then we set its MIME type to text/plain and the browser transformation to text/plain: dateformat. The next step is to edit the row for the 'Future souvenirs' book, and enter 2003-01-01 14:56:00 in the date_published field. When we browse the table, we now see the field formatted. Moving the mouse over the field reveals the unformatted original contents:

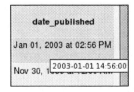

This transformation accepts two options. The first is the number of hours that will be added to the original value (by default, this is zero). Adding the number of hours can be useful if we *store* all the times based on **Universal Coordinated Time (UCT)** but want to *display* them for a specific zone (UCT+5). The second option is the time format we want to use, made from any PHP `strftime` parameters. So, if we put this in the transformation options, '0','Year: %Y', we will get:

Links from Text

Suppose that in our books table, we have put inside the description field of a row a complete URL: `http://domain.com/abc.pdf`. The text of the link would be displayed while browsing the table, but we would not be able to click it. We'll now see the use of the text/plain MIME type in such a situation.

text/plain: link

In the scenario we just mentioned, by using a MIME type of text/plain and a browser transformation of text/plain: link, we will still see the text of the link, but it will be clickable:

If all the documents that we want to point to are located at a common URL prefix, we can put this prefix (for example, `http://domain.com/`) in the first transformation option, with the enclosing quotes. Then in each cell, we would only put the last part of the URL (`abc.pdf`).

A second transformation option is available for setting a title. This would be displayed in Browse mode instead of the URL contents, but a click would nonetheless bring us to the intended URL.

If we use only the second transformation option, we have to put quotes where the first option is to be entered, as follows: `''`,`'this is the title'`.

text/plain: imagelink

This transformation is similar to the previous one, except that we place in the cell a URL that points to an image. This image will be fetched and displayed in the cell along with the link text. Although the image here is stored on the local server, it could be anywhere on the Web.

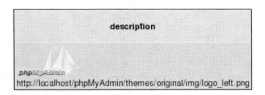

The first available option is the common URL prefix (like the one for text/plain: link), the second option is the width of the image in pixels (default: 100), and the third is the height (default: 50).

Because the link may refer to any browser-supported image type, which is not necessarily covered by phpMyAdmin's thumbnail generation mechanism, the image is just resized according to the options. To see the original image, we can click the link.

Preserving Original Formatting

Normally, when displaying text, phpMyAdmin does some escaping of special characters. For example, if we enter This book is good in the description field for one book, we would normally see This book is good when browsing the table. If we use the transformation text/plain: formatted for this field, we get the following while browsing:

In this example, the results are correct. However, other HTML entered in the data field could produce surprising results (including invalid HTML pages). For example, because phpMyAdmin presents results using HTML tables, a non-escaped </table> in the data field would ruin the output.

Displaying Parts of a Text

The text/plain: substr transformation is available to display only a part of the text. Here are the options:

- First: where to start in the text (default: 0)

- Second: how many characters (default: all the remaining text)
- Third: what to display as a suffix to show that truncation has occurred (default: ...)

Remember that $cfg['LimitChars'] is doing a character truncation for every non-numeric field, so text/plain: substr is a mechanism for fine-tuning this field-by-field.

External Applications

The transformations that have been described previously are implemented directly from within phpMyAdmin. However, some transformations are better done via existing external applications.

The text/plain: external transformation enables us to send the cell's data to another application that will be started on the web server, capture this application's output, and display it at the cell's position.

This feature is only supported on a Linux or UNIX server (under Microsoft Windows, output and error redirection cannot be easily captured by the PHP process). Furthermore, PHP should not be running in safe mode, so the feature might not be available on hosted servers.

For security reasons, the exact application path and name cannot be set from within phpMyAdmin as a transformation option. The application names are set directly inside one of the phpMyAdmin's scripts.

First, in the phpMyAdmin installation directory, we edit the text_plain__external.inc.php file in libraries/transformations/, and find the following section:

```
$allowed_programs = array();
$allowed_programs[0] = '/usr/local/bin/tidy';
$allowed_programs[1] = '/usr/local/bin/validate';
```

> The names of the transformation scripts are constructed using the following format: the MIME type, a double underscore, and then a part indicating *which* transformation occurs.

Each allowed program must be described here, with an index number starting from 0, and its complete path. Then we save the modifications to this script, and put it back on the server if needed. The remaining setup is completed from the same panel where we were choosing transformation options for other browser transformations.

Of course, we choose text/plain: external in the transformations menu.

As the first option, we place the application number (for example, 0 would be for the tidy application). The second option holds the parameters we need to pass to this application. If we want phpMyAdmin to apply the htmlspecialchars() function to the results, we put 1 as the third parameter (this is done by default). We could put a 0 there to avoid protecting the output with htmlspecialchars().

If we want to avoid reformatting the cell's lines, we put 1 as the fourth parameter. This will use the NOWRAP modifier, and is done by default.

External Application Example: In-Cell Sort

This example shows how we can sort the text contents of one cell. We start by modifying the text_plain__external.inc.php script, as mentioned in the above section, to add the sort program:

```
$allowed_programs[2] = '/bin/sort';
```

Note that our new program bears the index number 2.

Then we add a TEXT field to our books table: the keywords field, and we fill the MIME-related information:

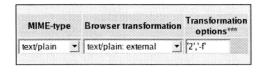

The '2' here refers to the index number for sort, and the '-f' is a parameter for sort, which makes the program sort uppercase and lowercase characters *together* instead of sorting uppercase characters *before* lowercase.

Next we Edit the row for the book *A hundred years of cinema (volume 1)*, entering some keywords in no particular order and hitting Go to save:

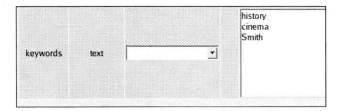

To test the effects of the external program, we browse our table and see the sorted in-cell keywords:

title	page_count approximate	author_id see authors table	language	description	cover_photo	genre	keywords
A hundred years of cinema (volume 1)	600	1	en		[BLOB - 0 Bytes]		cinema history Smith

Indeed, the keywords are displayed sorted in this cell, and the -f option has put the uppercase S of Smith in the correct order.

Summary

In this chapter we have seen how we can improve the browsing experience by transforming data, using various methods. We can:

- See thumbnail and full-size images of .jpeg and .png BLOB fields
- Generate links and format dates
- Display only parts of texts
- Execute external programs to reformat each cell's contents

Character Sets and Collations

This chapter explains how phpMyAdmin stores and fetches our data and how it deals with the character set and collation features available under MySQL. The program's behavior highly depends on the MySQL version used.

A **character set** describes how symbols for a specific language or dialect are encoded. A **collation** contains rules to compare the characters of a character set—more on this in the *MySQL 4.1.x and Later* section in this chapter.

The character set used to *store* our data may differ to the one used to *display* it, leading to data discrepancies. Thus, a need for transforming the data arises.

Language Files and UTF-8

UTF-8 is an encoding scheme to represent Unicode characters (see http://www.unicode.org). Unicode currently supports more than 600 languages, which is the main benefit of using it instead of other character sets from ISO or Windows, especially in a multi-language product like phpMyAdmin.

Note that the browser must support UTF-8 (most of the current browsers do). The phpMyAdmin distribution kit includes a UTF-8 version of nearly every language file in the lang subdirectory, and some of them are only available in UTF-8 encoding.

Some files are also coded using ISO or Windows character sets, with the goal of supporting older browsers, or because we don't have a UTF-8 converted version for those languages at the moment.

The possibility to choose a UTF-8 language file in the Language selector depends on the phpMyAdmin version used, the MySQL version, and—before phpMyAdmin 2.6.0—on some settings of config.inc.php.

Versions of MySQL Prior to 4.1.x

For versions of MySQL before 4.1.x, phpMyAdmin cannot rely on MySQL to transform the data according to the desired character set, because this feature does not exist in these MySQL versions. So, the actual recoding is done directly by phpMyAdmin, both before sending data to the MySQL server and after receiving it.

Data Encoding

For the actual encoding of data, the PHP server must support the `iconv` or the `recode` module. If this is not the case, the following error message will be generated:

Can not load iconv or recode extension needed for charset conversion, configure php to allow using these extensions or disable charset conversion in phpMyAdmin.

If this message is displayed, consult your system's documentation (PHP or the operating system) for the installation procedures.

Before phpMyAdmin 2.6.0, the default `config.inc.php` file did not make use of UTF-8 encoding: the `$cfg['AllowAnywhereRecoding']` parameter was set to `FALSE`. Thus, no UTF-8 languages were offered in the **Language** selector. To enable it, we just changed the parameter to `TRUE`.

In phpMyAdmin 2.6.0, the parameter is still set to `FALSE` by default, but the UTF-8 language choices are nevertheless displayed in the **Language** selector. This situation may lead to encoding problems—see *The Impact of Switching* section in this chapter.

Another parameter, `$cfg['RecodingEngine']`, specifies the actual recoding engine (the choices being `auto`, `iconv`, and `recode`), but we can leave it to `auto` unless we prefer to directly specify the one to use. With `auto`, phpMyAdmin will first try the `iconv` module, and then the `recode` module.

Character Sets

When considering the available choices, we should understand that, when connected to a pre-MySQL 4.1.x server, phpMyAdmin has limited support for character-set conversion. Currently we can specify which character set applies to a query and its results. The character set used by default is defined in the following parameter.

```
$cfg['DefaultCharset'] = 'iso-8859-1';
```

This is only the default choice; users may always select another character set from the choices listed in this parameter (the actual parameter in `config.inc.php` contains more):

```
$cfg['AvailableCharsets'] = array(
    'iso-8859-1',
    'iso-8859-2',
```

```
'iso-8859-3',
'iso-8859-4');
```

These choices are displayed to users in the same order as that defined in the parameter $cfg['AvailableCharsets']. So, we can move the most popular choices to the top. Any character set supported by the iconv or recode recoding engines may be used.

Let's say that we are using phpMyAdmin 2.6.0, but $cfg['AllowAnywhereRecoding'] has been left to its default FALSE value. This means that on the Home page we see:

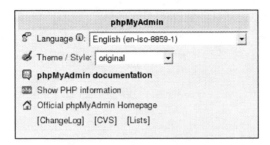

There is no MySQL Charset selector. The character set defined in $cfg['DefaultCharset'] will be used to communicate with MySQL.

Choosing the Effective Character Set

Now, we set $cfg['AllowAnywhereRecoding'] to TRUE. Then we choose English (en-utf-8) in the Language selector. The Home page has changed:

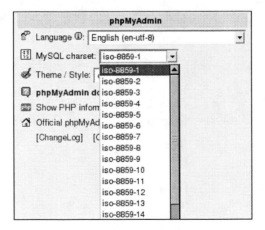

The MySQL Charset choice appears only if the current chosen Language uses UTF-8 encoding. From now on, every communication that occurs between the web server and the MySQL server will use this MySQL character set.

This choice of character set is remembered—for a period of thirty days—using a cookie mechanism. Hence, depending on the exact place the cookies are stored—on the local computer or on a network server—the character set could have to be chosen again if we log in to phpMyAdmin from another computer.

The Impact of Switching

When we choose a character set, all the data stored in MySQL will be recoded with this character set, so we will get incorrect results when fetching this data if we subsequently change the character set used by phpMyAdmin. There is no easy way of finding *which* character set was used to store a particular row of data.

Here is an example with our authors table. We first create a new author with a character é in his name:

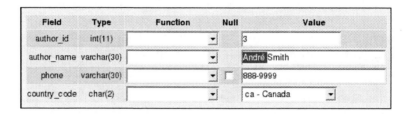

No problem here for inserting, browsing, or searching for this new author, as the chosen character set iso-8859-1 can deal with the é character.

If suppose we later decide to switch (on the Home page) the MySQL Charset to utf-8, we see a problem while browsing the authors table:

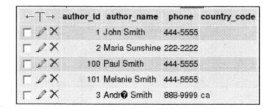

The same problem occurs—in phpMyAdmin 2.6.0—if we switch from one character set to another on the Home page, when our $cfg['AllowAnywhereRecoding'] is set to FALSE. Thus it is highly recommended to avoid switching character sets if our system is not configured to do the necessary conversion.

Importing and Exporting with Character Sets

If $cfg['AllowAnywhereRecoding']$ is TRUE, then on pages where a query box appears, the Location of the textfile dialog is modified to add the choice of character set for the file to be imported:

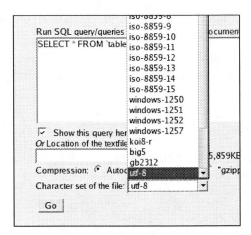

In the Export dialog, we can also choose the character set of the file to be created:

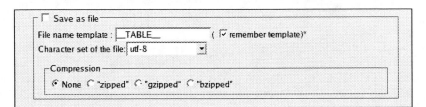

MySQL 4.1.x and Later

Since MySQL 4.1.x, the MySQL server does the character recoding work for us. Also, provisions have been made in MySQL to be able to indicate the character set and collation for each database, table, and even field. A default character set for a database applies to each of its tables, unless overridden at the table level; the same principle applies to every field.

In the current version of phpMyAdmin (2.6.0), support for MySQL 4.1.x character set and collation features is no longer experimental, as it was in previous versions.

The $cfg['AllowAnywhereRecoding']$ parameter has no impact for MySQL version 4.1.x and later.

Collations

When comparisons must be made between characters, precise rules must be followed by the system (MySQL in this case). For example, is 'A' equivalent to 'a'? Is 'André' equivalent to 'Andre'? These rules are called collations.

A proper choice of collation is important to obtain the intended results when searching data, for example from phpMyAdmin's Search page.

For an introduction to collations, see `http://dev.mysql.com/doc/mysql/en/Charset-general.htm`, and for a more technical explanation of the algorithms involved, refer to `http://www.unicode.org/reports/tr10/`.

Home Page

Here is what the Home page looks like, when connecting to a MySQL 4.1.x server (the sections that follow detail the changes):

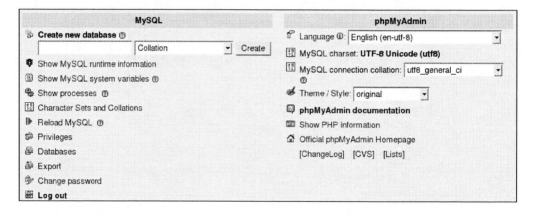

Create Database

When creating a database, we can choose its default character set and collation with the Collation dialog. This setting can be later changed (see the section *Database View*).

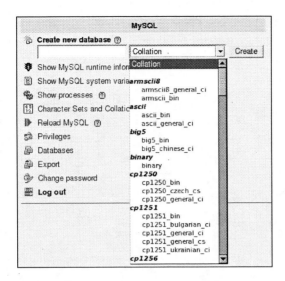

Available Character Sets and Collations

From the Home page, the Character Sets and Collations link opens the Server view on the Charsets sub-page, listing which character sets and collations are supported by this MySQL server. The default collation for each character set is shown with a different background color (using the row-marking color defined in $cfg['BrowseMarkerColor']):

Character Sets and Collations

Server: localhost

| Databases | Status | Variables | Charsets | Privileges | Processes | Export |

Collation	Description	Collation	Description
armscii8 (ARMSCII-8 Armenian)		**latin2** (ISO 8859-2 Central European)	
armscii8_general_ci	Armenian, case-insensitive	latin2_bin	Central European (multilingual), Binary
armscii_bin	Armenian, Binary	latin2_croatian_ci	Croatian, case-insensitive
ascii (US ASCII)		latin2_czech_cs	Czech, case-sensitive
ascii_bin	West European (multilingual), Binary	latin2_general_ci	Central European (multilingual), case-insensitive
ascii_general_ci	West European (multilingual), case-insensitive	latin2_hungarian_ci	Hungarian, case-insensitive
big5 (Big5 Traditional Chinese)		**latin5** (ISO 8859-9 Turkish)	
big5_bin	Traditional Chinese, Binary	latin5_bin	Turkish, Binary
big5_chinese_ci	Traditional Chinese, case-insensitive	latin5_turkish_ci	Turkish, case-insensitive
binary (Binary pseudo charset)		**latin7** (ISO 8859-13 Baltic)	
binary	Binary	latin7_bin	Baltic (multilingual), Binary
cp1250 (Windows Central European)		latin7_estonian_cs	Estonian, case-sensitive
cp1250_bin	Central European (multilingual), Binary	latin7_general_ci	Baltic (multilingual), case-insensitive
cp1250_czech_cs	Czech, case-sensitive	latin7_general_cs	Baltic (multilingual), case-sensitive
cp1250_general_ci	Central European (multilingual), case-insensitive	**macce** (Mac Central European)	
		macce_bin	Central European (multilingual), Binary

Effective Character Set and Collation

phpMyAdmin picks the 'effective' character set—which is the one we want to see in our browser—that best fits our selected language. So on the Home page, we see, for example:

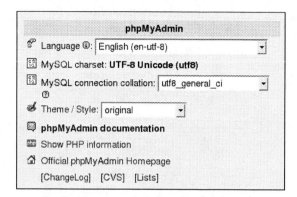

This character set information (as seen here in MySQL charset) is passed to the MySQL server, asking MySQL to transform the characters sent to our browser into this character set, and interpret accordingly what is received from the browser. Remember that all tables and fields have a character set information describing how the data is encoded.

We can also choose which character set and collation will be used on our *connection* to the MySQL server with the MySQL connection collation dialog. Normally, the default value should work, but if we are entering some characters using a different character set, we can choose the proper character set in this dialog.

> If a character does not exist in the chosen language, MySQL sends a question mark to replace it; for example, the author's name is André Smith and the chosen language is Bulgarian (bg-win1251), which doesn't have the é character.

Database View

In Database view, we can also change the default character set for the database:

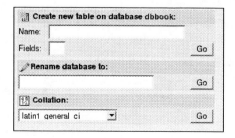

On the Structure page for a database, we now see the Collation used for each table:

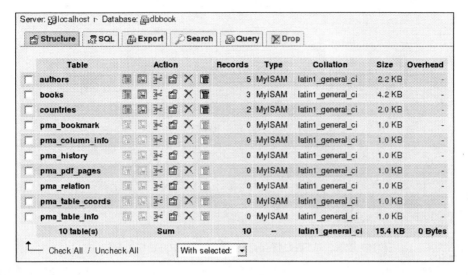

Table View

In the Table view's Operations sub-page, we can change the default character set and collation information for the table (see the screenshot that follows):

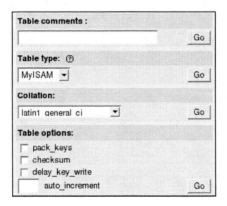

On the Structure sub-page Table view, we can also set the character set for each column:

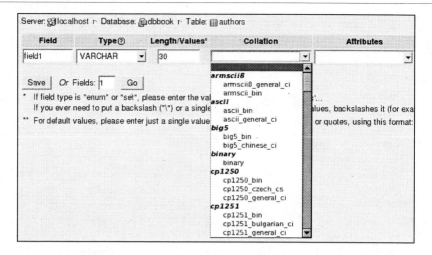

Importing and Exporting with Character Sets

In the export results, we can see the DEFAULT CHARSET and COLLATE information for the table and its columns:

```
CREATE TABLE `authors` (
  `author_id` int(11) NOT NULL default '0',
  `author_name` varchar(30) collate latin1_general_ci NOT NULL
default '',
  `phone` varchar(30) collate latin1_general_ci default NULL,
  `country_code` char(2) collate latin1_general_ci NOT NULL default
'',
  PRIMARY KEY  (`author_id`)
) ENGINE=MyISAM DEFAULT CHARSET=latin1 COLLATE=latin1_general_ci;
```

Server View

In the Server view, we can obtain statistics about the databases (see the *Database Information* section in Chapter 18). When our server supports character sets and collations, we see an additional information column, Collation, on this page:

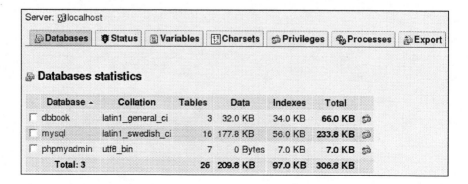

Kanji Support

If phpMyAdmin detects usage of the Japanese language, it checks if PHP supports the mb_convert_encoding() multi-byte strings function. If available, additional radio buttons are displayed to choose between EUC-JP and SJIS Japanese encodings on some pages:

- export
- insert text from a file
- query box

Summary

In this chapter, we covered:

- The use of language files in phpMyAdmin, including UTF-8
- The way phpMyAdmin has to recode our data in MySQL before its version 4.1.x
- The impact of switching from one character set to another
- The character set and collation features of MySQL, starting version 4.1.x

MySQL Server Administration with phpMyAdmin

This chapter will discuss how a system administrator can use phpMyAdmin server management features for day-to-day user account maintenance, server verification, and server protection.

Entering the Server View

From the Home page, the Server view can be accessed when we choose one of the following links:

- Show MySQL runtime information
- Show MySQL system variables
- Show processes
- Privileges
- Databases
- Export

The above links are visible only if we are logged in as a privileged user. When in the Server view, we see a menu to go to the other server-related sub-pages.

User and Privileges Management

The Privileges sub-page in the Server view contains dialogs to manage MySQL user accounts, and their privileges on global, database, and table levels. This sub-page is centered on the user and is hierarchical: for example, when editing a user's privileges, we can see his or her global as well as database-specific privileges. Then we can go deeper (for a database) to see table-specific privileges for *this* database-user combination.

User Overview

The first page displayed when we enter the Privileges sub-page is the User overview. This shows all user accounts and a summary of their global privileges:

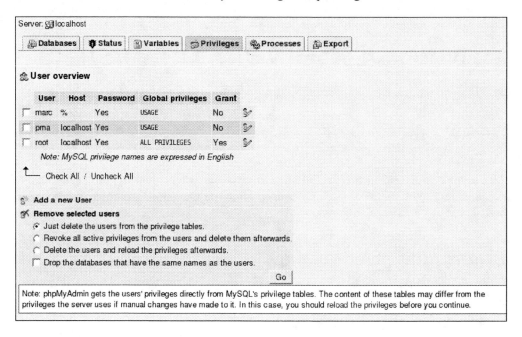

From this page we can:

- Edit a user's privileges with the Edit link on a user's line.
- Use the checkboxes to remove users with the Remove selected users dialog.
- Access the page where the Add user dialog is available.
- Reload the privileges. The effective privileges (the ones against which the server bases its access decisions) are the privileges that are located in the server's memory. Modifications to the privileges accomplished through phpMyAdmin's interface are made both in memory and on disk, in the mysql database. Modifications made directly on the mysql database do not have immediate effect. The Reload operation reads the privileges from the database and makes them effective in memory.

The displayed users' list has columns with the following characteristics:

- User: Users listed in an alphabetical order.
- Host: The host for which this user definition applies; a % value indicates all hosts. This is the machine name or IP address from which this user will be connecting to the MySQL server.

- Password: Contains Yes if a password is defined and No if it isn't. The current password value cannot be seen from phpMyAdmin's interface *or* by directly looking at the mysql.user table, as the password is obfuscated with a one-way hashing algorithm.
- Global privileges: Listed for each user.
- Grant: Contains Yes if the user can grant his or her privileges to others.

Add a User

The Add a new user link brings a dialog for user account creation:

Username

The User name menu offers two choices. Use text field enables us to input the new user name in the box right next to it, and Any user is there to create an anonymous user (the blank user). Let's choose Use text field and enter bill.

Host

By default, this menu is set to Any host, which would use % as the host value. The Local choice means localhost. The Use host table choice (which creates a blank value in the host field) means to lookup in the `mysql.hosts` table for database-specific privileges. Use text field allows us to input the exact host value we want. Let's choose Local.

Password

Even though it's possible to create a user *without* a password (with the No password choice), it's best to *have* a password. We have to enter it twice (as we cannot see what is entered) to confirm the intended password. Let's input bingo.

Global Privileges

Global privileges rule the access to all databases for this user, so they are otherwise known as superuser privileges. A normal user should not have any of these unless there are good reasons.

Of course, if we are really creating a superuser, we select every global privilege that is needed by this user. These privileges are further divided into Data, Structure, and Administration groups.

In our example, bill will not have any global privileges.

Resource Limits

We can limit the resources used by this user on this server (for example, the maximum queries per hour). Zero means no limit. We do not impose resources limits for bill.

The following screenshot shows the status of the screen just before hitting Go to create this user's definition (other fields have been left at their default value):

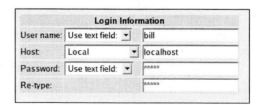

Edit a User

This page appears after a user's creation, or whenever we click Edit for a user in the User overview. There are four sections on this page, each with a distinct Go button, so each section is operated independently and has a distinct purpose.

Edit Privileges

This section has the same look as the one in the Add a new User dialog and is used to see and change global privileges.

Database-Specific Privileges

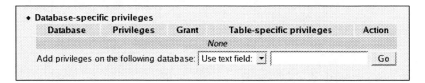

In this section we define the databases to which our user has access, and the exact privileges. Currently we see None because we haven't defined any. There are two ways of defining database privileges. First, we can choose one of the existing databases from the drop-down menu:

This assigns privileges to only this database. We can also choose Use text field and enter a database name. We could insert a non-existent database name here so that this user can create it later (provided we give him or her the CREATE privilege in the next panel), or we could use special characters like the underscore and the percent sign for wildcards.

For example, entering bill here would enable him to create a bill database, and entering bill% would enable the creation of any database that starts with bill. For our example, we will enter bill.

The next screen is used to set bill's privileges on the bill database and create table-specific privileges.

To learn more about the meaning of a specific privilege, we can move the mouse over a privilege name (which is always in English) and an explanation about this privilege appears in the current language. We give SELECT, INSERT, UPDATE, DELETE, CREATE, ALTER, INDEX, and DROP privileges to bill on this database, and click Go.

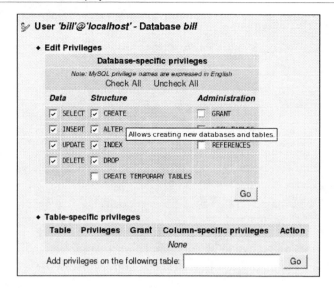

After the creation of privileges, the interface stays at the same place so that we can further refine the privileges. We cannot assign table-specific privileges for the moment because the database for which we created privileges does not exist.

The way to go back to bill's general privileges page is to click the 'bill'@'localhost' title:

This brings us back to the familiar page, except for a change in one section:

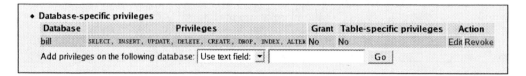

We see the existing privileges on the bill database for user bill (which we can Edit or Revoke), and we can add privileges for bill on another database. We also see that bill has no table-specific privilege on the bill database.

Change Password

This dialog is part of the Edit user page, and we can change bill's password or remove it, enabling a login without password for bill:

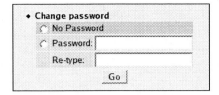

Change Login Information or Copy User

This dialog can be used to change this user's login information, or to copy the login information to a new user:

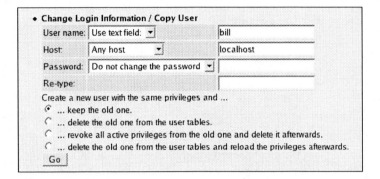

For example, suppose Bill calls and tells us that he prefers the login name billy instead of bill. We just have to add a y to the user name, choose Local as the host, and select delete the old one from the user tables:

After this operation, bill no longer exists in the mysql database, and all privileges will have been transferred to the user billy, including the privileges on the bill database. But bill's user definition still exists in memory, and so it is still effective. If we had chosen the delete the old one from the user tables and reload the privileges afterwards option instead, bill's user definition would immediately have ceased to be valid.

Alternatively, we could have created instead another user based on this user by making use of the keep the old one choice. We can choose to transfer the password to the new user, with Do not change the password, or change it by typing it twice. The revoke all active privileges option immediately terminates the effective current privileges of this user if he or she is logged in.

Remove a User

This is done from the User overview section of the Privileges page. We select the user to be removed, and then (in the Remove selected users) we use one of the following options, as appropriate:

- Just delete the users from the privilege tables: The deletion occurs only in on-disk definitions; effective in-memory user definitions are still working.

- Revoke all active privileges from the users and delete them afterwards: Delete effective in-memory privileges before removing them.

- Delete the users and reload the privileges afterwards: This option means that we don't have to remember to click the Reload the privileges link, which makes the deleted user's accounts non-functional.

We can also choose to Drop the databases that have the same name as the users.

Database Information

When we enter the Databases sub-page, we see the list of existing databases (with no accompanying statistics):

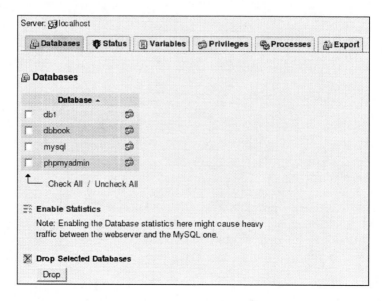

We also see an Enable Statistics link. By default statistics are not enabled because computing the size of data and indexes *for all tables of all databases* may cost valuable MySQL server resources.

Enable Statistics

If we click this link, a modified page appears:

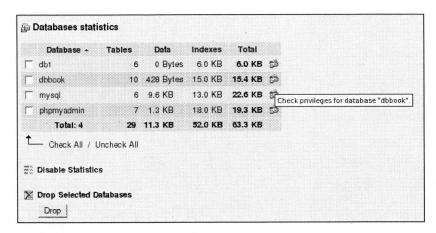

Sort Statistics

By default, the list is sorted by ascending database name. If we need to find the database with most tables, or one that takes the most space, a simple click on the Tables or Total column headers sorts accordingly. A second click changes the sort order.

Database Privileges Check

The Check Privileges link shows all privileges on a specific database. A user's global privilege might be shown here since it gives him or her access to this database as well. We can also see privileges specific to this database. An Edit link sends us to another page used to edit the mentioned user's privileges:

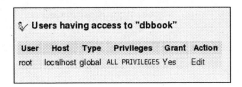

Drop Selected Databases

Here is an operation that should not be taken lightly. To drop some databases, we check the boxes next to the databases to drop, and use the Drop Selected Databases link. A confirmation screen follows.

Server Operations

The Status, Variables, and Processes links are available to get information about the MySQL server or to act upon specific processes.

Server Status Verification

These statistics reflect the MySQL server's total activity, including (but not limited to) the activity generated by queries sent from phpMyAdmin.

General Status Page

The Status link produces runtime information about this server. The page has several sections. First we get information about the elapsed running time and startup time, and then the total and average values for traffic and connections (the ø means average):

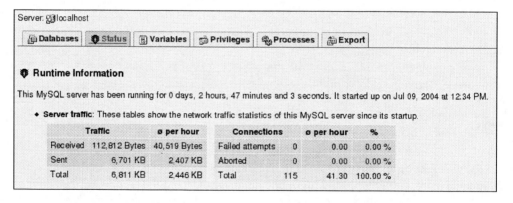

Next the statistics about queries are displayed (shown here partially). The average number of queries per hour, minute, and second give a good indication of the server load.

This is followed by statistics about each MySQL command, with the absolute number of times, hour average, and the percent of the total number of commands that a specific command was executed.

• **Query statistics**: Since its startup, 2,515 queries have been sent to the server.

Total	ø per hour	ø per minute	ø per second
2,515	903.32	15.06	0.25

Query type	ø per hour	%	Query type	ø per hour	%
admin commands	0	0.00	0.00 %	repair	0	0.00	0.00 %
alter table	8	2.87	0.33 %	replace	0	0.00	0.00 %
analyze	0	0.00	0.00 %	replace select	0	0.00	0.00 %
backup table	0	0.00	0.00 %	reset	0	0.00	0.00 %
begin	0	0.00	0.00 %	restore table	0	0.00	0.00 %
change db	1,038	372.82	43.25 %	revoke	2	0.72	0.08 %
change master	0	0.00	0.00 %	rollback	0	0.00	0.00 %
check	0	0.00	0.00 %	savepoint	0	0.00	0.00 %
commit	0	0.00	0.00 %	select	691	248.19	28.79 %

The next section presents other server information (again, shown partially):

• **More status variables**

Variable	Value	Variable	Value	Variable	Value
Created tmp disk tables	0	Open files	8	Ssl finished connects	0
Created tmp tables	5	Open streams	0	Ssl accept renegotiates	0
Created tmp files	0	Opened tables	166	Ssl connect renegotiates	0
Delayed insert threads	0	Qcache queries in cache	0	Ssl callback cache hits	0
Delayed writes	0	Qcache inserts	0	Ssl session cache hits	0
Delayed errors	0	Qcache hits	0	Ssl session cache misses	0
Flush commands	1	Qcache lowmem prunes	0	Ssl session cache timeouts	0
Handler commit	0	Qcache not cached	0	Ssl used session cache entries	0
Handler delete	0	Qcache free memory	0	Ssl client connects	0
Handler read first	6	Qcache free blocks	0	Ssl session cache overflows	0
Handler read key	30	Qcache total blocks	0	Ssl session cache size	0

InnoDB Status

On servers supporting InnoDB, a link appears at the end of the Status page, and when clicked, gives information about the InnoDB subsystem, including the last InnoDB error that occurred:

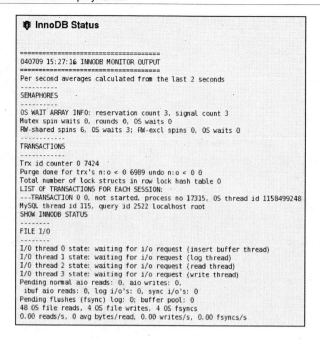

```
# InnoDB Status

========================================
040709 15:27:16 INNODB MONITOR OUTPUT
========================================
Per second averages calculated from the last 2 seconds
----------
SEMAPHORES
----------
OS WAIT ARRAY INFO: reservation count 3, signal count 3
Mutex spin waits 0, rounds 0, OS waits 0
RW-shared spins 6, OS waits 3; RW-excl spins 0, OS waits 0
------------
TRANSACTIONS
------------
Trx id counter 0 7424
Purge done for trx's n:o < 0 6989 undo n:o < 0 0
Total number of lock structs in row lock hash table 0
LIST OF TRANSACTIONS FOR EACH SESSION:
---TRANSACTION 0 0, not started, process no 17315, OS thread id 1158499248
MySQL thread id 115, query id 2522 localhost root
SHOW INNODB STATUS
--------
FILE I/O
--------
I/O thread 0 state: waiting for i/o request (insert buffer thread)
I/O thread 1 state: waiting for i/o request (log thread)
I/O thread 2 state: waiting for i/o request (read thread)
I/O thread 3 state: waiting for i/o request (write thread)
Pending normal aio reads: 0, aio writes: 0,
 ibuf aio reads: 0, log i/o's: 0, sync i/o's: 0
Pending flushes (fsync) log: 0; buffer pool: 0
48 OS file reads, 4 OS file writes, 4 OS fsyncs
0.00 reads/s, 0 avg bytes/read, 0.00 writes/s, 0.00 fsyncs/s
```

Server Variables

The Variables sub-page displays various settings of the MySQL server, which can be defined in, say, the my.cnf MySQL configuration file. These values can't be changed from within phpMyAdmin:

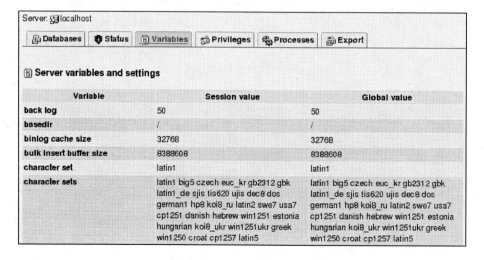

Server: localhost

| Databases | Status | Variables | Privileges | Processes | Export |

Server variables and settings

Variable	Session value	Global value
back log	50	50
basedir	/	/
binlog cache size	32768	32768
bulk insert buffer size	8388608	8388608
character set	latin1	latin1
character sets	latin1 big5 czech euc_kr gb2312 gbk latin1_de sjis tis620 ujis dec8 dos german1 hp8 koi8_ru latin2 swe7 usa7 cp1251 danish hebrew win1251 estonia hungarian koi8_ukr win1251ukr greek win1250 croat cp1257 latin5	latin1 big5 czech euc_kr gb2312 gbk latin1_de sjis tis620 ujis dec8 dos german1 hp8 koi8_ru latin2 swe7 usa7 cp1251 danish hebrew win1251 estonia hungarian koi8_ukr win1251ukr greek win1250 croat cp1257 latin5

Server Processes

The Processes sub-page is available to superusers and normal users. A normal user would see only processes belonging to him or her, whereas a superuser sees all processes.

This page lists all active processes on the server, and a Kill link that allows us to terminate a specific process.

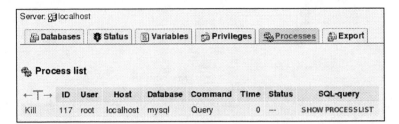

This example has only one running process, created by the SHOW PROCESSLIST command (done to generate this page), and so this one is not killable because it did not last long enough. We would normally see more processes running on a server with more activity.

Full Server Export

Chapter 7 explained how to export a database or a table. It is possible for a superuser or a normal user to export at least one or more databases in one operation.

The Export link brings us to the screen shown on the following page, which has the same structure as the other export pages, except for the databases list:

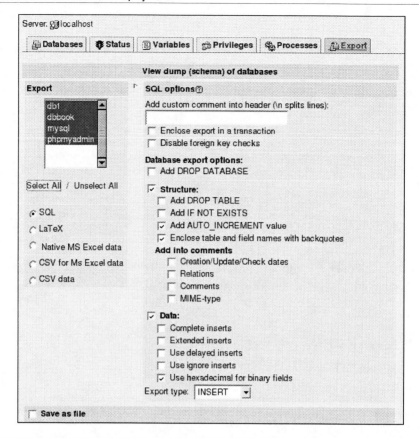

Exporting large databases may or may not work: this depends on their size, the options chosen, and the web server's PHP component settings (especially memory size and execution time).

Summary

In this chapter, we have seen various features available for system administrators:

- User account management
- Privileges management
- Database privileges check
- Server status verification
- Full server export

Troubleshooting and Support

This chapter proposes guidelines to solve common errors and gives hints to avoid problems. It also explains how to interact with the development team for support, bug reports, and contributions.

System Requirements

At the beginning of the Documentation.html file, which is included with the downloaded kit, a section discusses system requirements for the particular phpMyAdmin version we are using. It is crucial that these requirements be met and the environment be properly configured so that problems are avoided.

Some symptoms that may appear like phpMyAdmin bugs are in fact caused by the server environment. Sometimes, the web server is not configured to interpret .php files correctly, or the PHP component inside the web server does not run with the mysql extension. MySQL accounts may be badly configured. This can happen on home servers as well as hosted servers.

When we suspect that something is wrong, we can try a simple PHP script, test.php, which contains the following to check if the PHP component answers correctly:

```php
<?php
echo 'hello';
?>
```

We should see the hello message. If this works, we can try another script:

```php
<?php
phpinfo();
?>
```

This script displays information about the PHP component, including the available extensions. We should at least see a section about MySQL (proving that the mysql extension is available), which gives information about the MySQL Client API version.

We can also try other PHP scripts that make a connection to MySQL, to see if the problem is more general than just phpMyAdmin not working. As a general advice, we should be running the latest stable versions of every component.

Base Configuration

We should always double-check the way we made the installation, including proper permissions and ownerships. Typos may occur when modifying `config.inc.php`.

Solving Common Errors

To help solve a problem, we should first pinpoint the origin of the error message. Here are the various components that can generate these messages:

- MySQL server: These messages are relayed by phpMyAdmin, which displays MySQL said followed by the message
- PHP component of the web server (for example, Parser error)
- The web server itself (the error can be seen from the browser, or in the web server's log files)
- Web browser (for example, JavaScript errors)

The *Error Messages* and *Other Problems* sections were mostly based on various messages found on phpMyAdmin's help forum, and are also an expansion of material found in the FAQ section of `Documentation.html`.

Error Messages

This section refers to explicit error messages, as displayed by phpMyAdmin.

Cannot Load MySQL Extension

To connect to a MySQL server, PHP needs **MySQL extension**—a set of MySQL functions. This extension may be part of the PHP server (compiled-in) or may need to be loaded dynamically, but phpMyAdmin tried to load it and failed. This error implies that no other PHP script can make connections to a MySQL server.

The required extension is contained in a file that can be named `mysql.so` on Linux and UNIX, or `mysql.dll` on Windows. If our PHP server comes from a software package, we can find and install another software package probably called `php-mysql` (the name is distribution dependent). Otherwise, we can compile our own PHP server with the appropriate extension, as explained in the PHP documentation. At least one well-known Linux distribution (RedHat 8.0) fails to offer this extension as part of the web server/PHP server installation dialog, although the package is present on installation disk 3.

MySQL Said: Can't Connect to Local MySQL Server

This message indicates that the MySQL server is not running or cannot be reached from the web server. It can be also a socket (Linux/UNIX) or named pipe (Windows) configuration problem.

Socket Problem (Linux / UNIX)

The socket configured in php.ini (an example of which is given below) does not correspond to the socket of the running MySQL server:

```
mysql.default_socket = /tmp/mysql.sock
```

As a result, PHP cannot reach MySQL. We can change it to:

```
mysql.default_socket = /var/lib/mysql/mysql.sock
```

However, to be sure, we must find the exact location of this socket.

Named Pipe Problem (Windows)

A problem similar to the above, but on Windows can be solved by adjusting mysql.default_socket, but this time with the correct named pipe used to connect locally to a MySQL server. For example:

```
mysql.default_socket = MySQL
```

Error # 2003: The Server is not Responding

If the MySQL server is not on the same machine as the web server and is not answering, phpMyAdmin—starting with version 2.6.0—detects the fact and reports it accordingly.

MySQL Said: Access Denied

This error can be solved when we understand the relevant login parameters.

When Using http Authentication

We cannot use the web server security mechanism based on a .htaccess file, *and* the http authentication in config.inc.php together. A workaround is to use cookie as the authentication type instead of http.

When Using http, cookie, or config Authentication

The host parameter in config.inc.php must match the host defined in the user access privileges. Sometimes, a system administrator may create an account authorizing user bill and host localhost. If we try to use 127.0.0.1 host in config.inc.php, it will be rejected by MySQL even though it points to the same machine. The same problem can occur if we try the real name of the machine (mysql.domain.com) and the definition has been made for localhost.

Access Denied ... "using password: NO"

If the message ends with using password: NO, it means that we are not transmitting a password, and MySQL is rejecting this login attempt. The password value may not have been set in config.inc.php.

Access Denied ... "using password: YES"

A password is transmitted, but the host/username/password combination has been rejected by MySQL.

Warning: Cannot Add Header Information

This problem is caused by some characters—like blank lines, spaces, or other characters that are present in config.inc.php—either before the <?php tag at the beginning, or after the ?> tag at the end. We should remove these with an editor that supports .php files, as discussed in Chapter 2.

MySQL Said: Error 127, Table Must Be Repaired

In the left panel, we click on the database name, select the table name (using the relevant checkbox) on which there is an error, and choose Repair from the lower dropdown. More details are available in Chapter 10.

BLOB Column Used in Key Specification without a Key Length

MySQL requires that an index set on a BLOB column be limited in size. Since the simple index creation technique available when creating a column does not permit the size to be specified, the correct way to do is to create the column without an index, and then come back to the Structure page and use the Create an index dialog. Here we can choose the BLOB column and set a size for the index.

IIS: No Input File Specified

This is a permission problem. **Internet Information Server (IIS)** must be able to read our scripts. As the server is running under the user IUSR_*machinename*, we have to do the following:

- Right-click on the folder where we installed phpMyAdmin
- Choose Properties
- Under the Security tab, click on Add and select the IUSR_*machinename* user from the list
- Ensure that this user has read permission to the directory

A "404: page not found" Error when Modifying a Row

This happens when our $cfg['PmaAbsoluteUri'] parameter in config.inc.php is not set properly. Chapter 2 explains how to take care of this parameter.

Other Problems

Here we cover solutions to problems that do not show up on screen as a specific error message.

Blank Page or Weird Characters

By default, phpMyAdmin uses output buffering and compression techniques to speed up the transmission of results to the browser. These techniques can interfere with other components of the web server, causing display troubles. We can set $cfg['OBGzip'] to FALSE in config.inc.php. This should solve the problem.

Not Being Able to Create a Database

On the Home page, No privileges appears next to the Create database dialog if phpMyAdmin detects that the account used to log in does not have the rights to create a database. This situation occurs frequently on hosted servers, where the system administrator prefers to create one database for each customer.

If we are not on a hosted server, this message simply reflects the fact that we do not have the global CREATE privilege.

Problems Importing Large Files or Uploading Large BLOBs

Usually, these problems indicate that we have hit a limit during the transfer. Chapter 8 explains these limits and the recommended course of action. As a last resort solution, we might have to split our large text files (search on the Internet for **file splitters**).

MySQL Root Password Lost

The MySQL manual explains the general solution at
http://www.mysql.com/doc/en/Resetting_permissions.html.

The solution involves stopping the MySQL server, restarting it with the special option—**skip-grant-tables** (which basically starts the server without security). The way to stop and restart the server depends on the server platform used. Then we can connect to the server from phpMyAdmin as a superuser (like root) and any password. The next step is to change root's password (see Chapter 17). Then we can stop the MySQL server and restart it using normal procedures (security will become active again).

Duplicate Field Names when Creating a Table

Here is a curious symptom: when we try to create a table containing, for example, one field named FIELD1 of type VARCHAR(15), it looks like phpMyAdmin has sent a command to create two identical fields named FIELD1. The problem is not caused by phpMyAdmin but by the environment. In this case, the Apache web server seems well configured to run PHP scripts when in fact it is not. However, the bug only appears for some scripts.

The problem occurs when two different (and conflicting) sets of directives are used in the Apache configuration file:

```
SetOutputFilter PHP
SetInputFilter PHP
```

And

```
AddType application/x-httpd-php .php
```

These sets of directives may be in two different Apache configuration files, and so they are difficult to notice. The recommended way is to use AddType, so we just have to put comments on the other lines, as shown in the following snippet, and restart Apache:

```
#SetOutputFilter PHP
#SetInputFilter PHP
```

Authentication Window Displayed more than Once

This problem occurs when we try to start phpMyAdmin with a URL other than the one set in $cfg['PmaAbsoluteUri']. For example, a server may have more that one name, or we may be trying to use the IP address instead of the name.

Column Size Changed by phpMyAdmin

MySQL itself sometimes decides to change the column type and size, for a more efficient column definition. This happens mostly with CHAR and VARCHAR.

Seeing many Databases that Are Not Ours

This problem occurs mostly after an upgrade to MySQL 4. The automatic server upgrade procedure gives the global privileges CREATE TEMPORARY TABLES, SHOW DATABASES, and LOCK TABLES to all users. These privileges also enable users to see the names of all the databases (but not their tables) until we upgrade the grant tables as described in the MySQL manual. If the users do not need these privileges, we can revoke them, and they will only see the databases to which they are entitled.

Not Being Able to Store a Value Greater than 127

This is normal if we have defined a column of type TINYINT, since 127 is the maximum value for this column type. Similar problems may arise with other numeric column types. Changing the type to INT expands the available range of values.

Seeking Support

The starting point for support is the home page http://www.phpmyadmin.net, which has sections about documentation and support (feedback). There you will find links to the discussion forums, and to various trackers, such as:

- Bugs tracker
- RFE (requested features) tracker
- Translations tracker
- Patches tracker
- Support tracker

FAQ

The Documentation.html file, which is part of the product, contains a lengthy FAQ section, with numbered questions and answers. It is recommended to peruse this FAQ section as the first source for help.

Help Forums

The development team recommends that you first use the product's forums to search for the problem encountered, and then start a new forum discussion before opening a bug report.

Creating a SourceForge Account

Creating a (free) SourceForge user account and using it for posting on forums is highly recommended. This enables better tracking of questions and answers.

Choosing the Thread Title

It is important to carefully choose the summary title when we start a new forum thread. Titles like "Help me!", "Help a newbie!", "Problem", or "phpMyAdmin error!" are difficult to deal with because answers are threaded to this title and further reference becomes problematic.

Reading the Answers

As people will read and almost always answer our question, giving feedback in the forum about the answers can really help the person who answered, and others who have the same problem.

Support Tracker

This is another place to ask for support. Also, if we have submitted a bug report, which is in fact a support request, the report will be moved to the support tracker. With your SourceForge user account, you will be notified of this tracker change.

Bug Tracker

In this tracker, we see bugs that are not yet fixed, plus bugs that have been fixed for the next version (this is to avoid getting duplicate bug reports).

Environment Description

Since developers will be trying to reproduce the mentioned problem, it helps to describe our environment. This description can be short but should contain the following items:

- phpMyAdmin version (the team, however, expects that it is the current stable version)
- Web server name and version
- PHP version
- MySQL version
- Browser name and version

Usually, specifying the operating system on which the server or the client are running is not necessary unless we notice that the bug pertains to only one OS. For example, FAQ 5.1 describes a problem where the user could not create a table having more than 14 fields. This happens only under Windows 98.

Bug Description

We should give a precise description of what happens (including any error message, the expected results, and the effective results we get). Reports are easily managed if they describe only one problem per bug report (unless the problems are clearly linked).

Sometimes, it might help to attach a short export file to the bug report to help developers reproduce the problem. Screenshots are welcome.

Contributing to the Project

Since 1998, hundreds of people have contributed translations, code for new features, suggestions, and bug fixes.

The Code Base

The development team maintains an evolving code base from which they periodically issue releases. In the home page downloads section, a paragraph describes how to use CVS to get the latest version in development (this can be also done by downloading the CVS snapshot). A contribution (translation update, patch, new feature) will be considered with a higher priority if it refers to the latest code base, and not to an ancient phpMyAdmin version.

Translation Updates

Taking a look at the project's current list of 47 languages, we notice that they are not equally well maintained. We can try to join the official translator of a particular language to propose corrections or translations of the last added messages. If this person does not answer, we can send our modifications to the translation tracker, inside a compressed (.zip) file.

Patches

The development team can manage patches more easily if they are submitted in the form of a context diff against the current code base, with an explanation of the problem solved or the new feature achieved. Contributors are officially credited in Documentation.html for their work.

Future phpMyAdmin Versions

Here are the features that the development team is considering for possible implementation:

- Improved support of MySQL 4.1/5.0's new features
- db-based configuration with user preferences
- PHP sessions support
- Expand the product to support other database systems

Summary

In this chapter:

- We saw how to prevent troubles with a properly configured server
- We explained common errors, with suggested solutions
- We saw where to ask for help
- The *Contributing to the Project* section explained how to help in order to improve phpMyAdmin

Index

D

PACKT
PUBLISHING

More *solutions* Less *wasted time*

Learning eZ publish 3

Leaders of the eZ publish community guide you through this complex and powerful PHP based content management system.

- o Build content rich websites and applications using eZ publish
- o Discover the secrets of the eZ publish templating system
- o Develop the skills to create new eZ publish extensions

Building Websites with the ASP.NET Community Starter Kit

A comprehensive guide to understanding, implementing and extending this powerful and free application from Microsoft.

- o Learn .NET architecture through building real-world examples
- o Understand, implement and extend the Community Starter Kit
- o Learn to create and customize your own website
- o For ASP.NET developers with a sound grasp of C#

Building Websites with OpenCms

A practical guide to understanding and working with this proven Java/JSP based content management system.

- o Understand how OpenCms handles and publishes content to the Web
- o Learn how to create your own complex, OpenCms website
- o Develop the skills to implement, customize, and maintain an OpenCms website

Content Management with Plone

A comprehensive guide to the Plone content management system for Plone website administrators and developers.

- Design, build, and manage content rich websites using Plone
- Extend Plone's skins and content types
- Customize, secure and optimize Plone websites

Business Process Execution Language for Web Services

An architect and developer's guide to orchestrating web services using BPEL4WS.

- Specification of business processes in BPEL
- BPEL and its relation to other standards
- Advanced BPEL features such as compensation, concurrency, scopes, and correlations
- The Oracle BPEL Process Manager and BPEL Designer
- The Microsoft BizTalk Server 2004 as a BPEL server

SpamAssassin: A practical guide to Configuration, Customization, and Integration.

An in-depth guide to implementing antispam solutions using SpamAssassin.

- Detect and prevent spam using SpamAssassin
- Install, configure, and customize SpamAssassin
- Integrate SpamAssassin with major mail agents and antispam services
- Use SpamAssassin to implement the best antispam solution for your network and your business requirements

Building Websites with Microsoft Content Management Server

A fast-paced and practical tutorial guide for C# developers starting out with MSCMS 2002.

- o Learn directly from recognized community experts
- o Benefit from rapid developer level tutorials
- o Develop a feature rich custom site incrementally
- o Receive professional tips and tricks from developer newsgroups and online communities

Visit **www.PacktPub.com** for information on all our books.

Printed in the United States
34967LVS00003BA